The Manager's Pocket Guide to

Corporate Culture Change

Organizational Performance

Workgroup Technology

Virtual Work

Richard Bellingham, Ed.D.

HRD Press, Inc. • Amherst • Massachusetts

Published by:

HRD Press
22 Amherst Road
Amherst, MA 01002
1-800-822-2801 (U.S. and Canada)
413-253-3488
413-253-3490 (FAX)
www.hrdpress.com

ISBN 0-87425-616-X

Cover design by Donna Thibault-Wong
Editorial services by Sally M. Farnham
Production services by Anctil Virtual Office

Printed in Canada

Table of Contents

This book is aimed at the intersection of organizational performance, workgroup technologies and virtual teams. This book explores the challenges of change in a virtual environment. It also discusses how workgroup technologies can enable successful change in that environment.

Introduction and Overview

Changing corporate culture cannot be a random activity. Leaders must take a logical and systematic approach to change in order to achieve desired results. While much has been written about the Seven Ss (shared values, strategy, structure, staff, systems, skill, style) depicted in the graphic below, we have found that most organizations do not follow a prescribed order. Some organizations attempt to renew their organizations through restructuring efforts. Others try to renew themselves through intensive skill training programs or educational seminars on style preferences and differences.

From our experience, we have found that the most successful change programs start with a statement of shared values. Starting with values ensures that the entire organization puts purpose before action. Then, effective organizations articulate well-developed strategies to accomplish the purpose. With well-defined values and a clearly articulated strategy, it is possible to make intelligent decisions about structure, staff, systems, skills, and style requirements, and to create a high purpose, high performance organization.

As you have seen from the Table of Contents, the first skill of changing corporate culture is to "mobilize people behind

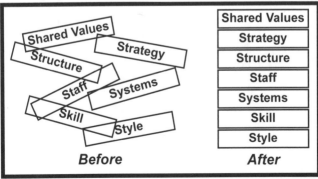

Before	After
Shared Values	**Shared Values**
Strategy	**Strategy**
Structure	**Structure**
Staff	**Staff**
Systems	**Systems**
Skill	**Skill**
Style	**Style**

the shared values, strategy and structure." While it is beyond the scope of this book to develop strategy or decide upon new organizational structures, we would be remiss not to discuss the critical importance of these key ingredients to renewal. Thus, this introduction will frame the Seven Ss in relation to changing corporate culture and then put the skills of this book in their proper context.

The Impact of Business Drivers on Strategy

We hear about it on TV, read about it in newspapers and magazines and talk about it formally and informally. By now, most people are aware that massive changes are taking place in the business world. The industrial age continues to give way to the information and electronic age. The factors creating these changes include:

- **The global village**—Businesses are being forced to compete in a global economy where competition for quality goods at competitive prices is coming from all corners of the world. The emerging economies are placing competitive pressure on companies as never before. As trade barriers crumble, opportunities and challenges are created. The global village is also creating a more culturally diverse work force. Through this diversity comes creative opportunity as well as challenge.

- **Customer-focused relationships**—The consumer's increasing demand for better quality means companies that are flexible and able to respond quickly to market changes will remain competitive. Today, the new challenge is to develop interdependent relationships with customers to provide tailored solutions for their specific problems and opportunities. This shift in relationship (from "order taker" to "partner") has imposed enormous new demands on organizations. We can no longer be content when our customer satisfaction ratings are high; we have to respond, personalize and initiate solutions that result in customer growth.

- **Faster pace**—The increasing development and availability of electronic communications technology, such as fax, telephone, modem, satellite transmission, Internet communication and computer software, are creating a faster-paced workflow with greater flexibility and less dependence on the traditional office concept. Product development and redesign cycles have become increasingly compressed. Faster has become the corporate mantra. We are the fastest generation on record. Anything that makes things happen faster is readily adopted and admired. Speed has become a major competitive factor.

- **Strategic collaboration**—Companies who were once bitter adversaries are shifting attitudes to a more cooperative existence when combining their strengths builds a better mousetrap than either could build separately.

All of these business drivers have a profound impact on strategy. In addition to all the other factors influencing strategy, these must also be taken into account when leaders develop their strategies for the future.

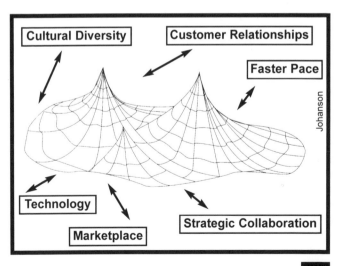

The Implications of Strategy on Structure

Organizations most likely to succeed during this storm of change are those willing to take a new look at the way they do business, particularly their work-force structure.

Traditional hierarchical corporate structure is permanent, structured and rigid. A new, more effective model is the Fishnet model created by Robert Johanson of the Institute for the Future. The Fishnet organization is flexible—able to form and reform various patterns of relationship among managers and workers. Events either external or internal that create challenges or opportunities are known as "spikes" in the Fishnet model. Companies respond to the spikes by building teams of diverse workers to reach the organization's immediate goals, then dismantle the team to create new teams. The Fishnet model allows for fluid redefining of roles and leadership, while retaining its strength and interconnections. This new model is gaining increasing acceptance because it is:

- Business driven rather than organizationally driven
- Dynamic and flexible
- Worldwide and cross-cultural
- Cross-functional
- Inter-enterprise

New Strategies and Structures Impose New Demands on Staff and Teams

Clearly, these changes in strategy and structure create new requirements on staff. People and teams must be able to relate to diverse cultures and style, to think interdependently and to plan for ever increasing time-to-market demands as they seek out opportunities to collaborate. In addition, new structures put demands on people and teams to manage multiple bosses, to communicate electronically with people all over the globe and to be flexible and adaptive.

The challenges of teams today are different from those of the recent past. Today, many teams are geographically dispersed. They may also come from different disciplines, departments or even different organizations. We call this type of team a *Virtual Team.*

The advantage of virtual teams is that there are no geographic or organizational boundaries. By using modern communication technology, virtual teams can bring the best and brightest individuals together without the cost and trouble of travel or relocation.

Teams today need to develop trust and collaborate in a virtual world. But trust and collaboration are difficult when people are physically separated for long periods of time.

The essential elements of high performing teams need to be developed among people all over the world, who may not know each other and who may work together on a team for only a few months. Creating high performing teams, therefore, not only requires a solid foundation on the basics of teamwork, but also requires enabling technologies to accelerate and sustain progress.

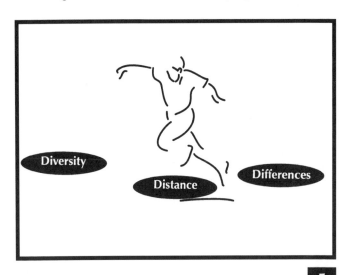

The Need for Robust Systems to Support the Structure

New strategies, structures, and staffing requirements create the need for adequate systems to support them. Many organizations now have Chief Information Officers (CIOs) to address the Information Systems (IS) requirements to enable all these changes. While this book cannot possibly overview all the IS changes taking place in organizations today, it will address the ways in which workgroup technology can enable changing corporate culture efforts.

Working without boundaries. Workgroup technology is a collection of computer software applications developed to allow individual team members to work together on projects regardless of geographic location. Workgroup technology generally works in tandem with the latest communication technologies, such as fax, modem, satellite transmission, laptop computers, E-Mail, etc. These technologies particularly enhance communication and interpersonal group activities. They cannot perform the tasks of a project, but they enhance and support the individuals working on a project from disparate locations.

Work anytime, anywhere. There are four basic time/space configurations for groups to work together using workgroup and communication technology.

- *Same Time/Same Place*—the traditional concept of meetings in which each member of the team comes together at a specific location and time.

- *Same Time/Different Place*—members meet together at the same time, but may be in different locations aided by technology such as telephone conference calling or video teleconferencing. Workgroup technology enhances this process by allowing more than one person to work on the same file at the same time from different locations.

- *Same Place/Different Time*—members work on the project within the same location but come and go at different times.
- *Different Time/Different Place*—members work on projects at different times and different locations using both workgroup and communication technology.

In the future the concept of any time/any place teamwork will increasingly provide flexibility and speed for bringing new products and services to the demanding marketplace at an ever increasing pace.

The new team technologies help virtual teams function, but a high performing team still requires strong team development skills to maximize the usefulness of the technology.

Additionally, the management of the communication continuum needs to be fluid and flexible. That is, knowing when to use a specific time/space configuration is key to managing team performance. Different points in the team process require different structures. The successful leader will be attuned to the needs of the team at each stage of development and adjust the communication model accordingly.

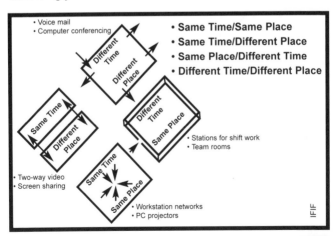

New Systems Require New Skills and Different Styles

As the changes inherent in the first five Ss cascade through the organization, people are compelled to learn new skills and to modify their styles. Many organizations are attempting to compare their current "skill profiles" with anticipated requirements for the future. Unfortunately, most skill profiling efforts do not take into account all the demands imposed by changes in shared values, strategy, structure, staffing and systems.

In addition to new skill requirements, changes in the way we do business have translated into new rules for interactions with associates, customers, competitors and partners. For example, workgroup and team technologies are designed to promote collaboration. Working together in collaboration can not only be a rewarding experience, but has traditionally facilitated some of the greatest human creations.

Although our society often rewards competition, it is through collaboration that some of the greatest scientific discoveries have been made. In fact, it has been said that competition chokes the creative process.

We define collaboration as two or more individuals with complementary skills working together to create a shared understanding that none had previously possessed or could have come to on their own (Schrage, 1990).

Where would Elton John have been without lyricist Bernie Taupin? Or Rodgers without Hammerstein?

Organizations that support and reward collaboration will meet the emerging challenges of change, taking advantage of the global economy, new technology and cultural diversity to bring better quality products and services to ever demanding customers.

The demands on leaders in the 21st century are ever increasing as they try to steer their organization through the turbulence of change happening in today's economic climate. How can we achieve business goals, keep our employees motivated and inspired and utilize emerging technologies all while we're navigating through continuous whitewater? The Seven Ss hold the key to helping leaders steer through the turbulence to achieve their goals.

We have found there are three key success factors in changing corporate culture efforts: commitment, capacity and culture. For any change to be successful, leaders need to have a simultaneous focus on all three factors. Renewing the organization through changes in values, strategy, structure, etc., requires broad commitment throughout the organization. Developing capacity accelerates the process, and aligning the culture sustains whatever changes are achieved.

	Commitment	Capacity	Culture
Shared Values			
Strategy			
Structure			
Staff			
Skill			
Style			
Systems			

The Need for Renewal

Well-established organizations may have particular difficulty recognizing and identifying the effects of the pressures of change and the need for renewal. The difficulties causing decline can take place slowly, go undetected, or be denied for years. If the organization is "lucky," a crisis may happen to shake things up enough to motivate change. For unlucky organizations the gravitational downward spiral may continue until the point of no return—orders are given: Do Not Resuscitate.

The National Aeronautics and Space Administration (NASA) was an organization suffering from years of decline masked by denial. The result of this denial was tragic. Seventy-three seconds into what had become a common launching of the space shuttle Challenger, a horrible explosion killing all seven crew members (including a public school teacher) was witnessed around the world. This event shocked the nation and severely damaged the public's confidence in the NASA space program. Twenty-five years after the first manned space flight, this crisis of monumental proportions shook the agency to its knees, forcing it to reflect and change, or cease to exist. NASA had once been considered an exemplary organization. But upon internal investigation it became clear that this exemplary organization was as vulnerable to human failure, misinterpretation of data, rigid adherence to routines that weren't working, poor communication, denial and stress as any organization large or small. Unfortunately it took a tragedy to get their attention.

NASA's story is a great example of an organization that, by drifting away from its primary focus, had fallen into decline and was badly in need of changing corporate culture efforts (Guy, 1989). Leaders, by necessity, must recognize, identify and discuss crises and opportunities before, during, and after they occur so that the organization believes there is sufficient urgency to change. Unless a large majority of people are truly convinced that the current "raft" will sink during the next whitewater, and unless radical changes are made, the end result will be denial . . . until doom strikes.

Renewal Begins

Once people accept the fact that business as usual is unacceptable, they begin to mobilize behind the changes. The question is "how" to mobilize people in a systematic way so that renewal efforts result in competitive advantage.

Leadership provides the substance of renewal. While all of these renewal tasks, discussed above, are requirements for growth, the leadership issue is central to success. John Kotter, Professor of Leadership at the Harvard Business School, asserts that forming a powerful guiding coalition— a team with enough power to lead the renewal effort —is an often ignored step in organizational transformation.

This book explores the challenges of change in a virtual environment. It also discusses how workgroup technologies can enable successful change in that environment.

This book is organized around four key tasks for renewal:
1. Maximizing Commitment
2. Building Capacity
3. Aligning the Culture
4. Managing Change

Leadership Behaviors
for Facilitating, Accelerating and Sustaining High Performance

Maximize Commitment — Mobilize, Empower, Recognize

Build Capacity — Develop, Learn

Align Culture — Articulate, Create

Manage Change
Understand • Accept • Enable

Task I.
Maximizing Commitment

Key Ingredients:
- Interdependent contract
- Inspiring visions

Critical Skills:
1. Mobilize people behind the values and vision
2. Empower people to control their work and life
3. Recognize individual and team contributions

We often hear organizations talk about people as the most valuable and valued asset, but we rarely see a consistent set of actions and initiatives that support those statements. In most organizations, that phrase is simply an empty slogan that causes more cynicism than commitment.

The unspoken contract between organizations and employees that once existed has been irrevocably breached. Downsizing, delayering, and restructuring within companies coupled with mergers and acquisitions between companies have profoundly changed the relationship between employee and employer.

In the book *Ethical Leadership* (Bellingham and Cohen, 1990), a series of five-point rating scales lets employers and employees assess their current relationship and identify possibilities for maximizing commitment. The scale for employee development is as follows:

1.0 Employees are given only the facts they need to know to do their jobs. They are largely ignored.

2.0 Employees are offered programs that give them a conceptual overview of their job, its function, the skills required to perform the job and how those skills contribute to the organization. They are informed.

3.0 Employees are equipped with an educational core set of skills designed to help them think better, relate more constructively and plan systematically. These skills empower employees to contribute to the organization. Employees are involved appropriately in decisions that affect them. They have access to and support to use discussion databases.

4.0 The generic skills of employees are reinforced with opportunities to learn and practice functional applications (for example: coaching, delegating and conducting performance reviews.) These are the skills required for success as a manager in any organization. The employees are incorporated into the business. The culture values the use of technology.

5.0 The organization educates its employees so that their street value meets or exceeds their compensation in their current job. By so doing, the organization reduces employees' fears about instability, insecurity and reductions in force because the employees know they can leave whenever the gap between their personal values and their job requirements is too large. What employees may lose in job security, they will gain in career security. At the same time, this type of psychological contract eliminates the pressure of employers to make lifetime employment guarantees. At level 5.0, the ethical organization is freed to achieve a realistic balance between satisfying worker values and meeting stockholder recommendations. Both the organization and the individual win through improved education. Employees are inspired to rally behind the vision and mission. The organization makes sure people have the skills and knowledge needed to use available technologies.

In the traditional organization, there was a dependent relationship in which security was rewarded for loyalty. In the 1980s that implicit contract became null and void. This resulted in an independent relationship in which each party's position was, "You take what you can get, and I'll take what I can get." The new emerging contract links developmental opportunities with organizational commitment. Developmental opportunities include training and support to utilize available technologies. It is an interdependent relationship in which both parties actively seek ways to help the other succeed, regardless of the length of the relationship. In making the transition from dependent loyalty to interdependent commitment, leaders need to acknowledge old expectations and articulate the new ones. Employees, on the other hand, need to take more responsibility for enhancing their own careers. Finally, both parties need to engage in open, honest discussions regarding organizational and individual expectations and how each can help the other achieve their goals.

Just as the "contract" has changed, the context has changed as well. While long tenure used to be viewed positively, in the 1990s a job history with a variety of companies was more valued. Given all these changes, what can a manager do to maximize commitment in the organization? Maximizing commitment is an absolute must for any organization to succeed in its renewal effort. Without it, valuable energy will be wasted. In his book, *Inspiring Commitment* (1995), Dr. Anthony Mendes discusses how to win loyalty in chaotic times. His book summarizes the literature on commitment and provides specific guidelines and principles for increasing it.

This section condenses some of the findings from his book into three key skills.

Skill 1. Mobilize people behind the shared values, strategy and structure.

Skill 2. Empower people to control their work and their life.

Skill 3. Recognize individual and team contributions.

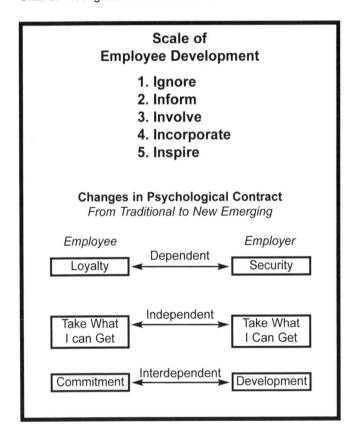

**Scale of
Employee Development**

1. Ignore
2. Inform
3. Involve
4. Incorporate
5. Inspire

Changes in Psychological Contract
From Traditional to New Emerging

Employee   *Employer*

Dependent
| Loyalty | ←→ | Security |

Independent
| Take What I can Get | ←→ | Take What I Can Get |

Interdependent
| Commitment | ←→ | Development |

SKILL 1:
MOBILIZE PEOPLE BEHIND THE SHARED VALUES, STRATEGY AND STRUCTURE

- **Definition:** Creating positive energy for change
- **Benefits:**
  — Higher productivity
  — Improved focus
- **Steps:**
  A. Define the core values and vision
  B. Align the structure with the strategy
  C. Engage people in the change

Introduction

Mobilizing people and teams behind the values, strategy and structure creates positive energy for change. When there is positive energy, people are able to produce more with less effort. When there is positive energy, people and teams use available technologies to communicate and participate. They are more focused on the possibilities and have an excitement about the renewal effort. Instead of wasting energy on complaints and negativity, there is an infectious vitality that enables people to focus on achieving business results.

There are three steps to mobilizing people behind the values, strategy and structure:

Step A. Define the core values and vision.
Step B. Align the structure with the strategy.
Step C. Engage people in the change.

The Virtual Challenge

The shift to a virtual environment has had a penetrating impact on how people are mobilized. Looking at the world as an amalgam of potential partnerships versus hostile competitors influences decisions about shared values, strategy and structure.

In a virtual environment, maximizing commitment poses a considerable challenge. How does a leader inspire people and create a sense of interdependence when members of the team are spread across the globe.

The Haelan Group, an Integrated Health Management Systems company headquartered in Indianapolis, exemplifies how a virtual company can deal with the commitment issue.

Haelan has affiliate partners who run independent businesses in several major cities around the world. In order to heighten commitment among the affiliate partners, Haelan held a worldwide conference in its early stages that involved all the partners in forming the shared values, strategy and structure.

Based upon input from all partners at that meeting, Haelan developed an affiliate partner agreement that specified expectations of all members. All the partners had ample opportunity to shape the agreement to meet their needs. Upon that base of involvement and clarity, Haelan is now able to communicate through a variety of modes to maintain high commitment among the partners.

Step A.
Define the core values and vision

- **What it means:**
    - Clarifying the ideal end state and what is most important for getting there.
- **How it works:**
    - Define three to five core values
    - Create an inspiring vision

The Idea

Values and vision inform strategy and structure. They establish purpose before action. Values and vision are different.

Values indicate what is important to the organization and guide how the organization conducts itself. Shared values are primarily directed toward process.

Core values should be shared by as many people as possible throughout the organization and among partners. Similarly, everyone in the organization should feel that their primary role is to contribute to the vision.

Implanting a set of core values into the organization helps the leadership and employees measure their decisions against well-defined criteria. The values become benchmarks for assessing success and a guidepost in the decision-making process.

Values should not be confused with operating principles. Generally they are limited to no more than five key values. Core values communicate what's important to the organization.

Much has been written about vision statements and mission statements. Essentially, a vision represents the ideal end state or the furthest implications of your work. A mission, on the other hand, simply describes the nature of your business. For example, a vision statement for a telecommunications firm might be "connecting civiliza-tions," while its mission statement might be "to be the leading manufacturer of digital switching equipment."

A vision statement should be passionate, short and powerful. At NASA, the early vision was to put a man on the moon before the Soviets. Every person in the organization was mobilized around that vision. This vision was so ingrained, that if an outsider were to ask the janitor what his or her job was, the reply would be, "To put a man on the moon before the Soviets."

We believe, incidentally, that defining the core values should precede the creation of a vision statement because the values represent who you want to be as an organization, while the vision statement defines what you want to become.

Beyond the values and vision, it is also critical to define the mission, goals, objectives, and strategies so that people share a clear understanding about the direction the organization is headed. While this exercise focuses on the first two essentials (values and vision), it may be useful for you to focus also on the more specific variables, depending on what you believe requires more clarity in your organization.

Including the use of technology within the values and vision statement of the organization sends a powerful message to employees about the commitment to and support of technology. It also provides a benchmark to ensure that the day-to-day operating functions are aligned with the values of technology.

Example

NASA's vision statement in 1986 was the same as it had been in 1958: to surpass the Soviets in space exploration, to impress the world with its feats, and trust that its work will enhance the lives of all Americans.

The changes in economic conditions and loss of public interest following the moon landings had resulted in serious budgetary restraints. Over time, NASA leaders were affected by these pressures and began changing the agency focus from safety and quality to maintaining funding.

Agency leadership allowed safety requirements to slide in order to meet budgetary constraints imposed by Congress. At the same time, the need to impress the public (to maintain funding) had manifested itself as an unrealistic launch schedule of 24 missions per year. This also compromised safety by not allowing enough time to correct problems when they were seen.

Many signals of safety problems were reported, but they were ignored in order to meet the schedule. Somehow the agency's personnel believed the values of the organization were quantity at low cost. The organization had lost its alignment with the values, vision, mission, goals, and objectives from the earlier years.

Today, NASA seems to have incorporated the budgetary constraints into their vision and mission. Engineers at the Jet Propulsion Laboratory in Pasadena, California, are being encouraged to find new technologies to bring the costs of missions down. Instead of trying to maintain the status quo by cutting corners, now they are using their considerable capabilities to find innovative ways to make the budget work.

Their mission now is to develop plans for small spacecraft that test new technologies to bring costs down. This change of values, strategies and vision has taken quite a bit of effort. But the scientists and engineers have had to change their thinking, or risk losing the space exploration program all together.

In the past, each mission was comprehensive and carried every conceivable instrumentation and every possible scientific experiment. The new projects are being scaled down. For example, a few years ago, engineers presented a new project based on the previous Jupiter explorer Galileo and Saturn explorer Cassini spacecraft model. The project would have cost $4 billion dollars. They were sent back to the drawing boards several times to come up with a way to bring the costs down. NASA officials call it "a deep cultural change."

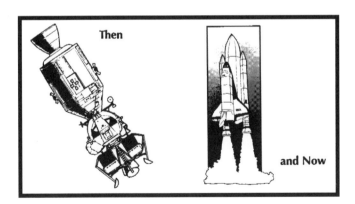

Then

and Now

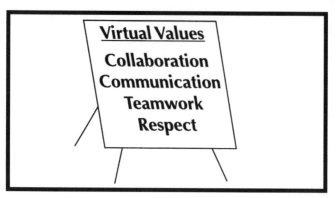

YOUR
TURN

Use the space below to list the core values in your organization.

How have value statements changed in the past years? What new words are appearing?

Are they the right values for a virtual environment?

Step B.
Align the structure with the strategy

- **What it means:**
  - — Align company around several core processes
- **How it works:**
  - — Assess the level of strategic and tactical clarity
  - — Decide on the best "engagement strategy"

The Idea

In the past, companies organized themselves in vertical structures to take advantage of functional expertise. In vertical, hierarchical structures, everyone understands where they fit in the organization and what their role is. Direction is clear because decision-making power resides at the top. Unfortunately, in this type of organizational structure, clarity is achieved at the expense of collaboration. In vertical organizations, most people don't understand the overall company objectives and strategies and how their work contributes to company and customer success.

In a horizontal structure the company is organized around several core processes with specific performance goals and ownership of each process. While organizations shift to this new structure, it is important not to make any significant structural changes until the strategy is well developed. The structure needs to support the strategy.

After the strategy is well-defined, then structural decisions need to be made around the hierarchy, processes, teams and customer goals. One option is to build the company more around processes than around functions or departments. Another option is to reduce layers of management and eliminate the work that fails to add value. A third option is to build the organization based on teams and let them manage themselves.

Examples

Eastman Chemical Co. replaced several functional vice presidents with self-directed work teams. It's organizational chart is called "the pizza chart" because it looks like a pizza with a lot of pepperoni sitting on it. It is represented in circular form so that everyone is equal in the organization.

McKinsey and Co. conceptualized the horizontal organization with a drawing of three boxes floating above a series of core processes. The circles represent the cross-functional nature of the teams in charge of the processes.

AT&T Network Systems Division has assigned "owners" and "champions" to 13 core processes. The owners are responsible for the day-to-day operations of a process, and the champions make sure that the process remains linked with overall business strategies and goals.

In this book we have highlighted the Fishnet model developed by the Institute for the Future. This model has advantages in today's world because it suggests that teams can mobilize nicely around changes in internal and external factors: customer needs, competitive threats, technological or economic trends, and changing values within the organization. The Fishnet model also recognizes a fundamental reality of today's global economy: on a moment's notice, companies may have to shift direction 180 degrees based upon new information in the marketplace.

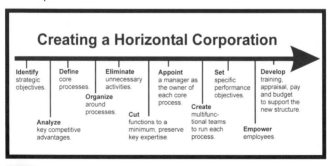

Creating a Horizontal Corporation

Identify strategic objectives.

Analyze key competitive advantages.

Define core processes.

Organize around processes.

Eliminate unnecessary activities.

Cut functions to a minimum, preserve key expertise.

Appoint a manager as the owner of each core process.

Create multifunctional teams to run each process.

Set specific performance objectives.

Empower employees.

Develop training, appraisal, pay and budget to support the new structure.

YOUR TURN

How has your organizational structure changed in the past several years? Is it now more vertical, more horizontal, or a hybrid?

What changes do you need to make in your organizational structure to ensure that it supports the strategy instead of encumbering the strategy?

Step C.
Engage people in the change

- **What it means:**
  — Linking individual vision to organizational vision
- **How it works:**
  — Encourage employees to create a meaningful
    mental picture
  — Describe the short-term and long-term goals
    and objectives for the organization
  — Align individual goals with organizational vision
  — Clarify responsibilities

The Idea

No matter how many times people and teams are told
about the values, vision, strategy and structure, the words
will have little meaning until each person has a chance to
discuss their personal and organizational significance and
implications. To be meaningful, organizational vision must
be linked to individual vision. Without individual vision,
commitment cannot take wing and elevate people to
greater heights. People need to engage in discussion
before they can understand, own, or internalize the
intended message. Getting alignment behind the vision
is the foundation for creating commitment.

Example

In the early years of NASA, safety was a primary value—
a benchmark that was used in the decision-making process. Safety was often the cause for delays in scheduled
missions. Somehow over the years, NASA was no longer
communicating its vision and values to employees; in
fact it appears that a set of unwritten values had taken
their place. On the morning of the Challenger launch,
temperature readings on the solid rocket booster were
below allowable safety standards. Launch personnel
ignored this because of the pressure to maintain the flight

schedule, and the now infamous explosion shortly after take off of Challenger resulted.

After this disaster, NASA was challenged to engage key leaders in a new discussion of the values and vision of safety and quality because of the decentralized nature of the organization. NASA has several centers around the country and many contractors. An effective communication plan to inoculate key leaders with the values of safety and quality might include all the key leaders from each division, the contractors, and even leaders of Congress. This task could be enhanced by using videoconferencing technologies that would facilitate discussion among many people in different locations.

The Virtual Challenge

A challenge of leadership in a virtual environment is to bring together disperse organizations with different targets under a common vision. Providing visible leadership in a virtual environment can be technically supported, but it also requires face-to-face meetings. In today's environment, some executives don't operate out of a corporate headquarters, so the new task is to create a virtual *Open Door.*

There are a number of strategies for communicating the values and vision (or mission, goals, objectives, strategies as the case may be) including teleconferences, open meetings, retreats, etc. Using these available technologies can help engage key leaders to participate, especially in a virtual environment. For example, creating an on-line question & answer database, using E-Mail and participatory log-on routines can be used to involve people in the process.

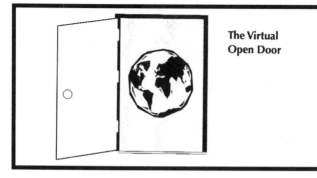

**The Virtual
Open Door**

YOUR TURN

*Which items on the following list are still unclear to people
in your organization? In the space below please develop
your program for engaging key leaders in a discussion of
the items you checked and how they impact the future
direction of your organization.*

Values

Vision

Mission

Goals

Objectives

Initiatives

Strategies

Your Program:

If you manage someone remotely, what is that person's perspective?

Develop an action plan for engagement. How will you determine how engaged people currently feel—particularly, those in the field? What options can you use to improve visibility?

SKILL 2:
EMPOWER PEOPLE TO CONTROL THEIR
WORK AND THEIR LIFE

- **Definition:** Sharing power and authorizing people to think and make decisions
- **Benefits:**
  — Encourages productive thinking
  — Frees initiative
  — Improves quality

$$E = D \times A \times S$$

- **Steps:**
  A. **D**efine job direction and boundaries
  B. Provide **A**utonomy to initiate within boundaries
  C. **S**upport people as needed

Introduction
Empowering means sharing power and authorizing people to think and make decisions (Carkhuff, 1989). Empowering requires that people have the skills they need to meet their responsibilities. In this Age of Information, empowering skills should emphasize processing information. Economists indicate that human and information capital have become the critical sources of economic growth.

"Empowering" is a term used in almost every corporation. Unfortunately for many, using the term has not translated into real behavior changes. For some, empowerment is cynically defined as, "I can do whatever I choose as long as it agrees with what my boss thinks." This misses the point in two critical ways. Empowerment does not mean anarchy or freedom to operate without limits, but it does mean thinking outside the box. Reconciliation of these two points is what causes tension around empowerment initiatives.

31

Empowerment is a process of balancing freedom with control so that all managers and associates accept responsibility and accountability. In addition, they are authorized, supported and recognized for their contributions.

Empowerment means that:

- Employees have the authority to make decisions that improve the quality of their work.
- Employees can make some improvements at work without first checking with their supervisor.
- Employees have significant control in their jobs.

Empowerment might include using technology to allow people or teams to work productively at home and providing them with flexible time. It might also include opening up information and giving people data, tools and the authority to use them to increase customer growth.

Thus, effective empowerment initiatives improve quality and commitment, free initiative, and give employees a greater sense of control. Leaders who want to make empowerment more than an empty slogan and want to avoid a cynical backlash think of this concept in terms of direction, autonomy and support. This skill will help you process those three dimensions of empowerment by taking three steps:

Step A. Define job direction and boundaries.
Step B. Give people autonomy to initiate within the boundaries.
Step C. Support people as needed.

The Virtual Challenge

Being able to process information more effectively requires constant access to information on which to base decisions. Portable technology enables easy and constant access to information as well as personal freedom and virtual participation. With this new technology, the boundaries between work and "personal life" have blurred. Just as employees can have access to information 24 hours a day, 7 days a week, bosses may also have access to employees 24 hours a day, 7 days a week.

Clearly, these technologies have positive and negative aspects. For example, with increasing freedom and distance from "headquarter environments," the notion of trust takes on new meaning. Who has access to what information? How often do we need to check in? Do we manage by results or manage by tasks?

Step A.
Define job direction and boundaries

- **What it means:**
  - Setting achievable goals and clarifying limits of authority
- **Steps:**
  - Establish agreed-upon stretch targets.
  - Communicate clear metrics and standards
  - Establish boundaries and transfer authority

The Idea

People and teams need to be clear about the limits of their authority, the problems they are trying to solve, and the goal they are trying to achieve. Without that understanding, empowerment results in random shots in the dark. For empowerment to work, people need to:

- Understand the company vision and direction;
- Know where they fit;
- Understand their roles and responsibilities;
- Understand the boundaries they operate within (e.g., service levels, fiscal constraints, decision-making authority);
- Accept accountability;
- Make decisions at the appropriate level;
- Feel free to speak up.

Some of the most useful steps leaders can take to define direction and boundaries are:

1. Establish agreed-upon stretch targets that align with the organizational vision.

2. Communicate clear measurements and standards for accountability, accomplishment and progress. Employees should, of course, participate in developing these measurements and standards.

3. Establish boundaries and transfer authority to accomplish the objectives.

The most useful boundaries are those that provide people and teams with general guidelines that they can use to make specific decisions.

The
Virtual
Challenge

Since teams are cross-functional, rapidly changing and more quickly disbanding, roles may not equal job descriptions. A person may have multiple roles and multiple bosses at the same time. The person someone reports to may not be the person who manages the actual task. The question then becomes, who defines the boundaries?

In a virtual environment, there are issues around individual boundaries and group boundaries. A team may have significant decision-making authority, but an individual within the team may not. With the movement toward shared responsibilities and accountabilities, the concept of boundaries is changing.

YOUR TURN

In the spirit of empowerment, what could you do to define the direction and boundaries for your employees?

Step B.
Provide autonomy

- **What it means:**
  - Enabling people to take control of their work and their life
- **How it works:**
  - Offer flexible work option
  - Provide opportunities for learning and development
  - Involve people in decisions that affect them
  - Challenge associates with meaningful work

The Idea
In an empowered organization, the leader may decide what needs to be accomplished and the associates decide how to get it done.

Providing people with clear boundaries is accomplished by what we talked about in the earlier sections. It means that employees have clear understanding of the values, vision, mission, goals, objectives and strategies that frame the work to be done. They are then given the autonomy to operate within those boundaries. With a clear understanding of the organizational values, they'll be able to make decisions that maintain consistency with the framework.

If we are going to take the notion of empowerment seriously, we need to consider the full context of the person's life. The goal is to empower people to take control of their life inside and outside of work. Implied in this goal is the recognition that people may have special needs at home, work, school, and in the community. Therefore, leaders who empower should:

- Provide employees with flexible home/work/school options made practical by the use of laptops, E-Mail and workgroup technology.
- Offer opportunities for learning and career enhancement, including technology training.
- Involve people in the goal-setting and decision-making processes, and give access to decision-making databases.
- Provide access to virtual meetings in which decisions are made.
- Challenge associates with interesting work.

Example

Nordstrom Department Store is a good example of an organization that has taken away hierarchical controls, shifted power to the employees and facilitated customer service in the process. Their policy and procedures manual is a single page, containing a single paragraph that simply tells employees to use their own judgment to help the customer in whatever way they can. Employees are empowered to use the resources of the store to solve customer problems.

NASA's communication structure did allow lower level staffers the autonomy to solve problems. It was structured so that if the lower level staffers couldn't solve a problem, it went up to the next level. If the higher levels didn't hear about it, it was assumed that the problem had been solved at the lower levels. Although this structure does empower staff members closest to the problem to get things done and have autonomy, it appears that the higher level managers had released too much control. When lower levels failed to pass the warning up the chain, the higher levels never got the signals of trouble and assumed that all was well. NASA's renewal strategy needs to include a checks and balances system where the upper level managers still have communication lines to the lower levels, while maintaining the autonomy of the lower levels.

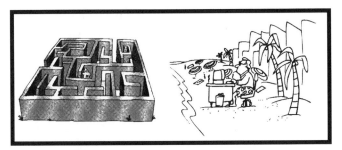

YOUR TURN

What ways could you free initiative within your organization in the following areas:

Flexibility:

Learning and development:

Involvement in decisions:

Meaningful work:

How do you make autonomy not look like neglect in a virtual environment?

How do you as a leader give up seeing what people are doing and still feel good about that?

What can you do to demonstrate that you are managing by results rather than by tasks or time?

Step C.
Support people as needed

- **What it means:**
  - Making discriminations regarding the amount of coaching, consultation, direction, and collaboration is required for each individual to succeed
- **How it works:**
  - Inform
  - Equip
  - Communicate
  - Resource

The Idea

Getting clear agreement on what needs to be accomplished and freeing people and teams to figure out how to get it done are two essential steps for empowerment.

The third step is to provide whatever support is needed to ensure they succeed with flying colors. This support includes the training and support for using technology.

Managers who are not comfortable with the notion of empowerment can undermine success by not being clear about objectives and withholding support. In effect, they set people up to fail.

Effective leaders make discriminations about how much support is needed. For some, delegation of the task is sufficient. Others may require significant coaching, consultation, specific direction or collaboration.

Another form of support involves providing the necessary resources. Does the team have the information, tools, technology, training and staff to accomplish the goal?

Clearly, from a leader's point of view, empowerment does not mean total withdrawal of involvement. On the contrary, empowerment requires clear directions and appropriate support, and it requires a clear definition of authority. Authority should be defined in terms of the power to enforce, decide and spend.

Example
One of the main problems facing many organizations, including NASA, is budget constraints. NASA would propose a program; Congress would cut the funding by one-third. This placed tremendous pressure on NASA leaders to provide the product (to receive favorable public opinion), but with fewer staff and resources.

With slashed budgets, NASA was struggling to maintain essential resources. It was reported that technicians pirated parts from one shuttle to fix another because they lacked a proper spare parts inventory. NASA leaders needed to ensure that the necessary resources were available. If budgets were cut by Congress, then the scope of the missions needed to be downsized as well.

Today, this is happening at NASA. NASA now openly acknowledges tough budgetary times. They know they can't fly missions at a billion dollars a pop. By reducing spacecraft weights, NASA is able to use less expensive rockets to launch new missions.

For example, instead of a traditional comprehensive mission to explore the planet Pluto at an estimated cost of $4 billion, NASA engineers came up with the Pluto Express to the tune of just $400 million. The Pluto Express is made up of two lightweight modules, incorporating microelectronic technologies. Additionally, they have reduced the amount of scientific instrumentation in each module. An increased amount of on-board automation will help reduce the costs of ground support.

Support Continuum

←———————————————————→

I'll tell you
everything
you need
to know

Here are the tools,
training, resources,
and authority to
figure out what
information you
need to get results

YOUR TURN

What are some of the ways you can support empowerment in your organization?

Communication:

Information:

Tools:

Staff:

Training:

Authorities:

Other:

SKILL 3:
RECOGNIZE INDIVIDUAL AND TEAM CONTRIBUTIONS

- **Definition:** Reinforcing valuable contributions
- **Benefits:**
    — Sustains positive behavior
    — Motivates high performance
- **Steps:**
    A. Define requirements and expectations
    B. Define the motivating factors for different groups
    C. Design a reward system

Introduction

Recognition is a way to reinforce valuable contributions. Stated objectives or new initiatives are unlikely to become a reality without reinforcement or incentive. Maximizing commitment is no exception to this. Like a car without gasoline, no matter how great it looks, it's not going anywhere. It is basic human nature to initiate and sustain behavior either to achieve a positive result or to avoid a negative one (Mendes, 1995). Also, as the unspoken contract between employer and employee changes from security to development, the fear of job loss or disciplinary action loses its power as a motivational tool.

Motivation is a primary concern of all organizations. Managers are constantly asking how they can get an employee and/or a team to want to do what needs to be done.

Motivation arises from people's beliefs about the consequences of their actions. If people or teams believe that the consequence of an action is favorable to them, then they will be motivated to perform.

45

Recognizing individual and team contributions is a key element of maximizing commitment and motivation. Successful reward and recognition programs must be:

- Tied to performance,
- Tied to employee values, and
- Based on achievable performance expectations (Bellingham and Cohen, 1989).

In this skill you will work through three steps for recognizing individual and team contributions:

Step A. Define requirements and expectations.
Step B. Define the motivating factors for different groups.
Step C. Design a reward system that is aligned with organizational and individual values.

The **V**irtual Challenge

We have always understood the importance of individual incentives. Now we must put as much brain power into the creation of appropriate team incentives as we have for individual incentives. Unfortunately, traditional models have reinforced the wrong behaviors for today's environment. For example, the traditional models reward individual accomplishment more than team accomplishment, and reward competitive behaviors more than collaborative behaviors.

In addition to shifting our emphasis from individual to team, we also need to focus on what types of incentives are useful in a virtual environment. While we still have to motivate individual behaviors, our incentives should be directed toward those behaviors that contribute to team effectiveness.

Step A.
Define requirements and expectations

- **What it means:**
  — Clarifying the criteria on which rewards and recognitions are based
- **How it works:**
  — Maintain an open system
  — Continually elicit input and feedback
  — Specify requirements before recognition and reasons after recognition

The Idea

People and teams need to be clear about the criteria on which they are being evaluated, rewarded, or recognized. If people know how a recognition system works prior to the giving of an award, they will be:

- More likely to perform at higher levels and
- Less likely to feel resentment or cheated if the reward goes to someone else.

Therefore, the first step in providing recognition is to define the requirements and expectations.

A productive organization tries to gain employee commitment to the requirements and expectations of the organization. This can be done by keeping an open system that continually asks for input and feedback in forming the corporate mission, goals, and objectives. That way, people may recognize their ideas represented in the mission and feel more invested in its success (Carkhuff, 1984).

Employees should always have access to these expectations and to past information regarding performance.

Example

NASA's expectations and requirements of staffers became severely skewed over a period of time. Where once safety and quality had been expected, now cost cutting, short cuts, and keeping schedules were the rewarded expectations. Part of this may have been caused by a shift in its primary mission of research and development for increasingly sophisticated space exploration to a mission of operating routine flights of commercial payloads. The requirements and expectations of an operating program of routine flights would by nature be different from those for research and development.

NASA needed to redefine its mission and align the requirements and expectations with that new mission. Involving all staff members in the development will help them commit to and understand the importance of these expectations.

Today, NASA has changed its definition of success. NASA's new proposed set of missions will still have scientific objectives, but its success will be judged primarily by how well the new lightweight, less costly technologies succeed.

These new technologies demonstrate that NASA has a different focus of getting costs down and increasing the frequency of space flight. These new missions are aligned with the need to have a publically visible program, but within the available funding constraints.

The Virtual Challenge

This step becomes more complex in a virtual environment, because it is sometimes unclear who is defining the requirements and expectations and how they fit with different organizational missions.

For virtual companies, when there are multiple bosses and a matrix organization, systematic planning models are imperative so that everyone is clear about how many days a month they are assigned to each individual.

With systematic planning, each person has a set of task cards that specify expectations with estimated time requirements per month. Therefore, if one of several bosses requests a person to perform additional tasks, the person can show the boss the set of cards and ask which one(s) the boss wants to eliminate. This process facilitates negotiation among bosses and between bosses and employees.

From an organizational perspective, we also need to define requirements and expectations with partners. In the Haelan Group, for example, a statement of work is outlined with each partner so that there is no confusion about conditions, terms, and stipulations.

YOUR TURN

How could you make the requirements and expectations of your organization more clearly defined and more widely understood?

How can you apply this step to motivation of team behaviors?

Step B.
Define the motivating factors for different groups

- **What it means:**
  - Differentially rewarding according to respective frames of reference
- **Steps:**
  - Define levels of performance within your group
  - Define levels of motivation
  - Explore the types of reinforcement that may be appropriate for the people in your group

The Idea

There are differences in values and levels of performance among individuals and groups. Reinforcement plans will be more effective if they recognize these differences and target specific employees' frame of reference. What motivates one type of performer may not motivate another. These strategies can be summarized in the chart on the next page.

According to this chart, detractors require close supervision and immediate dispensation of rewards. While observers may be able to respond to delayed incentives, they are motivated best by external rewards. Participants are best motivated to higher performance by understanding what their internal incentives are. Contributors are usually motivated by opportunities to pursue new learning that they can transform into working productively. Finally, exemplars are motivated by freedom and resources to pursue missions beyond management mandates (Carkhuff, 1984).

Corporate Culture Change

Team leaders can use this scale to improve levels
of functioning within the team. By diagnosing where
each member is on the scale, leaders can develop
individual improvement plans and elevate each
person's performance. It is especially important to
focus on those behaviors that lead to high team
performance, e.g., collaboration, cooperation, support,
respect, communication, etc.

This model can also be applied to how well people adopt
the use of technologies. Exemplars encourage, promote
and help others with the use of technology. Detractors
may promote negativity, sabotage, and hinder the use
of technology.

Levels of Performance	Levels of Motivation	Levels of Reinforcement
Exemplar	Mission fulfillment	Resources and responsibilities
Contributor	Self-actualization	Time and opportunity
Participant	Goal achievement	Internal incentives
Observer	Incentive	External incentives
Detractor	Non-incentive	Differential reinforcements

Carkhuff

YOUR TURN

Use the space below to list the different individuals and groups within your organization. Identify the key motivating factors for each of those groups.

Step C.
Design a reward system that is aligned with organizational and individual values

- **What it means:**
  - Tailoring reward conditions to what we say is important
- **Steps:**
  - Assess the gap between stated organizational values and what the reward system actually recognizes
  - Change the reward system in a way that reflects more congruence between organizational and individual values

The Idea

In most organizations, leaders "talk the talk, but don't walk the walk." This is because rewards are based primarily on short-term financial performance. While it is in vogue to talk about empowerment, involvement, open communications, trust, respect, fairness, balance, etc., the reward system rarely includes these aspects of leadership in any meaningful way. With the availability of 360-degree feedback systems where performance input comes from all levels surrounding an individual, it is now possible to measure these behaviors in a fair and accurate way. The question still remains, however, how much weight is given to the results of these feedback tools in recognizing individual and organizational performance?

Designing a reward system that is in harmony with organizational and individual values means tailoring our reward conditions to what we say is important. By doing so, it is possible to narrow the gap between stated values and principles and what people actually do (and get recognized for) in the organization.

Specifically, leaders need to reinforce team results as much as individual results. Leaders also need to reward innovation, collaboration and risk taking. In order to do this, leaders need to be open to systems that reward behaviors that may not pan out immediately. Expectations and norms that drive short-term thinking present barriers to implementing these types of systems.

Example
In a large research organization in the telecommunications industry, competitive pressures have forced dramatic changes in what gets rewarded. In the past, employees within this organization were rewarded for individual thinking and for conducting basic research. The reward system reflected a long-term investment strategy that tolerated years of research with no guarantees for results. The system, although costly and inefficient, produced a wide variety of patents that generated enormous revenues over a long period of time.

Changes in the marketplace have caused this organization to redesign its reward system so that it now reinforces interdependent relating and applied development with clear expectations for short-term product delivery. These changes have rocked the organizational culture and created individual and organizational turmoil. It is still unclear what impact these changes will have on the long-term health of this company.

In NASA's early days, if an employee had an accident resulting in damage, it was pardoned as long as the staffer fully reported the incident. This norm allowed problems to be brought into the open so corrective measures could be made. As pressures mounted to launch more and more missions, accidents resulting in a delay of the schedule were punished. Tension mounted as employees feared for their jobs. They responded by not communicating accidents or damage, and by "sweeping problems under the rug." Secrecy and denial were being rewarded in this system.

In the renewal effort, the agency needed to reinstate the policy of pardoning those who admit to mistakes. They also need to reward those who discover problems. If they rewarded personnel who "blew the whistle on problems," it would send a clear message to all about the commitment to safety and quality assurance.

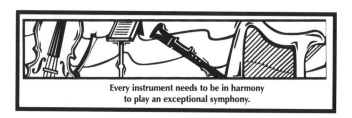

**Every instrument needs to be in harmony
to play an exceptional symphony.**

YOUR TURN

Use the space below to record what you can do to alter the reward system in your organization to make it more in agreement with organizational and individual values?

How can you reward innovation in the use of technology within your organization?

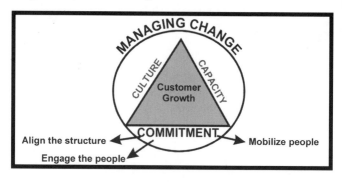

Task I. Commitment Exercise

In our task to maximize commitment, we have discussed three skills:

- Mobilize people behind the shared values, strategy and structure.
- Empower people
- Recognize individual and team contributions

Review these three skills and decide what actions you can take in your organization to maximize commitment.

Autonomy?

Empowerment?

Balance?

Trust?

Task I. Summary

To maximize employee commitment behind efforts to renew an organization, managers must first rally people around the new values and vision for the future. By defining the core values and vision, then engaging key leaders in the process, organizations can begin the process of making renewal efforts move forward in a positive way.

In the new organization, people need to be empowered to make decisions with autonomy, yet within clearly defined boundaries created by the vision, mission, goals, objectives and values. It is imperative at this stage of development that the organization provide people with the technical and human support necessary to get the job done.

Finally, in the goal of maximizing commitment, we cannot forget motivation and reward. Giving people specific expectations so that they know the basis for evaluation is a key part of a sound reward system. Understanding what motivates individuals within the organization and creating reward systems that are in tune with those motivators will ensure that employees are properly rewarded and motivated to work with the organization toward renewal.

All of these skills need to be performed in the context of a virtual environment. That means leaders need to consider the challenges of maximizing commitment in a dispersed organization in which trust, empowerment and balance take on entirely new meaning. The leader must also ensure that the reward system is sending the right messages around what behaviors are required in today's world. Specifically, the reward system must stop reinforcing too much individual competitiveness that undermines team performance and start reinforcing interdependent thinking, innovation and collaboration.

Task II.
Building Capacity

Key Ingredients:
- Customer focus
- People, products, processes, and technologies

Critical Skills:
4. Develop people
5. Create a learning organization

An organization may have the most committed people in the world, but capacity is still required to be successful. Building capacity means developing the people, products, processes and technologies to achieve customer growth.

Capacity development must be customer focused. Capacity-building efforts should ensure that processes are efficient and effective; that products meet customer requirements in timely ways; and that people have the skills, technology, and personal energy they need to do their jobs in the most effective ways. It is important to identify the technology appropriate for the task and provide proper training.

Capacity can be built on several levels. For mechanical capacity, an organization needs to have the hardware, equipment and tools to produce its product and provide services efficiently and effectively.

To build information capacity, organizations need the systems and software to process data in timely and meaningful ways.

An organization also requires sufficient financial capital to fund its investment and operating expenses.

At a generic level, another critical way to build capacity is to focus on human and organizational areas. This means developing highly energized, skilled, and enthusiastic people. Through continuous learning and active partnering your people will help the customer and each other succeed.

Developing the right products, engineering the right processes and selecting the right technologies is dependent upon our ability to learn from every transaction and from multiple sources. Therefore, this section will not attempt to be a primer for total quality, product development, re-engineering or technology selection. It will focus on people and organizational learning.

If an organization builds the capacity to learn from everything, quality products and processes will happen as a natural outcome. As a result, people will apply the information and technologies that are available to them. The failure of the past has been due to our thinking that an independent program, whether vertical or horizontal, could have an impact without interdependent thinking or leadership modeling.

This section will cover two skills:

Skill 4. Develop people.

Skill 5. Create a learning organization.

SKILL 4:
DEVELOP PEOPLE

- **Definition:** Creating an environment where there is a high level of satisfaction, empowerment and the optimal amount of stress
- **Benefits:**
  - Generates new sources of gain
  - Makes re-engineered processes successful
  - Creates the knowledge required to provide customer solutions
  - Gets people excited to come to work and reduces stress
- **Steps:** Attend to
  - A. Physical health
  - B. Emotional health
  - C. Intellectual health
  - C. Spiritual health

We want to develop people so that we can generate customer growth. Developing people has practical applications internally: develop quality products, engineer fine-tuned processes and leverage state-of-the-art technology. The question is "How does an organization build that capacity?"

Re-engineering business processes to achieve competitive advantage and organizational efficiency is sweeping through corporations worldwide. Equally important, but far less visible, is the need to revitalize the people and organizations that make re-engineered processes successful or not. Developing people represents the knowledge, skill, and capability of employees to provide solutions to customers. It is what people must know, do, and feel to be able to serve customers most effectively.

Senior managers should be leaders in developing and supporting policies and direction for all human and organizational wealth-building initiatives. People development integrates all of the programs and activities related to the generation of human and organizational wealth.

According to James Quinn of the Tuck School of Business at Dartmouth, even in manufacturing, three-fourths of value-added work derives from knowledge. The challenge is to learn how to operate and evaluate a business when knowledge is its chief resource and result.

And yet knowledge is just one dimension of developing people. Equally important are the physical, emotional, intellectual and spiritual (PEIS) processing skills that can continuously generate new sources of gain.

There are several programs available that are geared to each of these areas, but they usually operate in random, inductive and overlapping ways. If all of these initiatives were integrated and coordinated under a People Development strategy, the potential to create enormous organizational wealth would be greatly enhanced. Here are some examples of how current initiatives could be part of a comprehensive and systematic People Development strategy:

Physical Capital:
- Benefits
- Safety and Environment
- Health Promotion

Emotional Capital:
- Diversity
- Work/Life Balance
- Empowerment

Intellectual Capital:
- Education and Training
- Executive Development

Spiritual Capital:
- Sense of Community
- Volunteers for Service

Assuming that high performance and customer growth are the desired end states for a People Development strategy, leaders must address the key variables involved in creating high performing teams and organizations. According to the World Confederation of Productivity Science, the three most critical variables of high performance are:

- Satisfaction
- Control/Empowerment
- Stress/Challenge

The
irtual
Challenge

In a virtual world, it is more important to ask about satisfaction factors or survey people about them because the leader has fewer direct cues to indicate levels of satisfaction, control and stress. Leaders need to find explicit ways to keep a finger on the pulse of these critical factors.

Satisfaction	Control	Stress	Productivity Domain
High	High	High	Excited
High	Low	Low	Protected
High	High	Low	Relaxed
High	Low	High	Wonderment
Low	High	Low	Disdainful
Low	High	High	Angry/Used
Low	Low	Low	Depressed
Low	Low	High	Troubled

Generally, a person or team experiences job satisfaction when the activity of performing the work satisfies important values, e.g., variety, challenge, respect. Job satisfaction, when coupled with stress and control, is one of the best predictors of longevity and overall productivity. While very few people are perfectly content with their jobs, there are several statements that people who have the highest levels of job satisfaction usually make.

People with high levels of satisfaction say:

I make full use of my talents.
I feel good about what I am doing.
I am satisfied with my pay and benefits.
The pace and activity level is just right.
I feel involved in decisions that affect me.
I have the right amount of autonomy.
I am able to use my imagination.
I have opportunities for growth.
I am adequately recognized for good work.
My supervisor cares about me.
I have clearly defined goals.
My pay is linked to my performance.
I like the people I work with.
I am treated as a whole person with unique needs.

Similarly, the extent to which persons feel empowered to do their job determines their level of control. The most stressful jobs are those that have high demands but low control.

Not only do people who work in high demand/low control jobs experience more cardiovascular disease, but their performance suffers even before they experience a heart attack or disabling event.

When people feel empowered or experience control in their jobs, they typically make statements similar to these:

*I understand the vision, strategies, boundaries, and
    expectations for my job.*
I have the authority to carry out my responsibilities.
I am encouraged to take risks.
I am open to learning new technologies.
Mistakes are seen as opportunities to learn.
I am encouraged to think outside the box.
I am not micro-managed.
My manager trusts me.
My manager respects my opinion.
My manager shares power.
*I am authorized to think and make decisions at the point of
    need.*
*I have opportunities to learn the skills I need to function in
    an empowered way.*
I consider technology an enhancement to my work.
I experience more empowerment than control.
*Matrix management has increased the resources available
    to me.*
My work counts.
Ninety percent of my time is spent on productive work.

A feeling of control means that individuals can manage the demands on their time. In a virtual environment, this has unique ramifications. For example, the Fishnet organization means that multiple bosses may have multiple demands on a person's time. To complicate the matter further, in a technology-enabled, virtual environment with laptops and pagers, work can follow a person 24 hours a day, 7 days a week. On the other hand, some people, who prefer to work virtually, may appreciate the autonomy and flexibility in the way they manage their time.

The third variable is stress/challenge. Too much stress can cause the following types of symptoms:

Physical Symptoms
- Headaches
- Ulcers
- High blood pressure
- Insomnia

Mental Symptoms
- Confusion
- Forgetfulness

Behavioral Symptoms
- Irritability
- Impatience
- Shaking

On the other hand, insufficient stress can lead to boredom, depression or poor performance. The key to effective stress management is to match up demands with the resources available in a way that optimizes performance.

From a positive point of view, stress can breed community. People tend to increase their sense of connectedness when they are all experiencing challenging conditions.

A person usually experiences peak performance when they feel a high level of job satisfaction, a great sense of control and high challenge without excessive stress. The bulleted list above summarizes the effects on productivity and attitude for persons with variable levels of satisfaction, control and stress.

Developing people means creating an environment in which there is a high level of satisfaction, empowerment and an optimal amount of stress so that associates are excited about coming to work. In this skill you will create that environment by attending to the four developmental needs of employees:

Step A. Attend to physical health.
Step B. Attend to emotional health.
Step C. Attend to intellectual health.
Step D. Attend to spiritual health.

The **V**irtual Challenge

People who work in a virtual environment don't have the same opportunities for community and support as people who are co-located.

On the other hand, many people who work virtually don't have to face the same day-to-day stressors of their traditional counterparts. In many corporate settings today, most people experience a relentless intensity that may lead to stress overload.

Step A.
Attend to physical health

- **What it means:**
  - Recognizing and responding to signs of stress and needs for health
- **How it works:**
  - Identify signals of stress overload
  - Provide healthy food alternatives
  - Encourage exercise and fitness
  - Make work stations ergonomically sound

The Idea

Attending to physical health means recognizing and responding to signs of stress, providing healthy food alternatives at meetings, encouraging exercise and fitness, ensuring ergonomically sound work stations, and having a smoke-free environment. By doing this, employees generally experience higher levels of job satisfaction, feel more control in their lives, and are better able to handle stress.

Stress may even be created by having too much of a good thing. People can feel overloaded and stressed out when the technology outstrips their capability. For example, a person who was always ahead of schedule when the pace of work was done by hand, may now find themselves always behind schedule. This can create an image crisis where once the person was highly productive and received excellent reviews, now has trouble and is considered to be not as productive.

Leaders can play a major role in supporting health by setting a positive example and by supporting positive health practice. Unstated norms also play a crucial role in promoting physical health, For example, effective leaders:

- Don't schedule meetings at lunch if some participants use that time to exercise,
- Promote balance, and
- Are attuned to signs of stress overload.

Examples
Employees at NASA were under tremendous stress from knowing the level of safety risk being taken with each launch. One engineer, fearing the results of faulty O-rings, said he held his breath during every launch. Even if things were going well, NASA employees would be in a high stress environment just because the stakes are so high.

Return on Investment
A growing number of companies now understand that it pays to keep workers healthy. Recent studies show that for every dollar invested in preventive health care programs like Tenneco's, a company can save as much as six dollars in insurance costs *(Fortune,* 1995). Johnson and Johnson, for instance, which spends about $4.5 million a year on preventive health care programs, estimates its medical bills would be higher by $13 million a year (or 15 percent) without its wellness program. According to Mercer Inc. companies face a huge potential liability for high risk workers who are likely to be tomorrow's cardiac or cancer victims. By changing now, companies can hold down those future costs. Some examples are:

- Dow Chemical's Backs in Action program has decreased on-the-job problems by 90 percent.
- DuPont budgets $20 million a year to furnish tests and check-ups for employees.
- Quaker grants bonuses of as much as $500 for families who exercise, avoid smoking, and wear seat belts.

The Virtual Challenge

As a leader in a virtual environment, there are few opportunities to attend to the cues, demonstrate positive role modeling or establish healthy norms in the culture. And a person working in a virtual environment has fewer opportunities for support—a critical factor in any lifestyle behavior change.

Promoting health in a virtual environment must also include an awareness and concern for how the use of technologies creates stress and affects health. Are workstations ergonomically designed? Are workers encouraged to use the workstation in an ergonomically correct way? Is lighting adequate so as not to create eye strain? Does the technology function reliably? Being aware of the stressors created by technology and virtual environments is as important as understanding stressors from other factors.

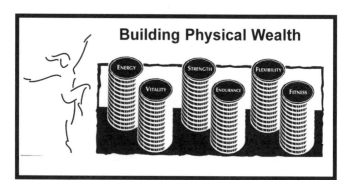

Building Physical Wealth

YOUR TURN

What are the signs of stress you are seeing in your organization?

What could you do to provide healthy food alternatives at meetings?

How could you encourage exercise and fitness?

What challenges does the virtual environment present for you?

Step B.
Attend to emotional health

- **What it means:**
  — Responding to unique needs and taking the
    initiative to support those needs
- **How it works:**
  — Support work/family balance
  — Deal effectively with conflict
  — Provide flexible work options
  — Communicate openly, directly and honestly
  — Be harder on yourself than you are on others

The Idea

Attending to emotional health means supporting work/
family balance, dealing effectively with conflict, providing
flexible work options and communicating openly, directly
and honestly. Again, all of these behaviors directly affect
employee satisfaction, sense of control and stress.

In today's world, fewer and fewer families conform to the
"traditional" structure of father working and the mother
staying home to raise the children and attend to civic
duties. For example, in the United States less than
11 percent of families are "traditional," and trends around
the world are following the same direction. Most families
today are either single-parent homes or dual-working
parents. This puts tremendous strain on the parents to
juggle home and work responsibilities while maintaining
energy to do both.

Working at home can be an opportunity to respond to this
dilemma. Leaders need to recognize, however, that people
need more freedom to work out suitable arrangements

for their particular situations. Whatever norms that are established in a given geography, leaders must take into account how those norms will play in different locations. For example the idea of balancing work and family in Japan is very different than the idea of balance in Europe.

Organizations drain productive energy from their workers by not dealing with conflict in a productive way or by communicating in a dishonest or secretive way. Just as employee theft drains an organization of financial capital, negative feelings drain a company of emotional capital. Conversely, of course, positive feelings toward work and the organization are a significant source of organizational wealth.

Examples
At AT&T, leaders responded to the needs of employees to balance home and family responsibilities by instituting a work/family program that provides time for employees to find appropriate care for their children and aging parents. This program was the result of union-management bargaining. It started with child care and then expanded to elder care in 1989.

Lines of open communication had deteriorated at NASA. Low level staffers were not passing bad news up the chain of command—only good news. And even when warnings were communicated, they were ignored. This sent a general message to all employees that dissenting opinions were not encouraged, particularly if it caused a delay in schedule. After the Challenger explosion, information and communications were completely clamped down for several hours. Associates with any involvement were ordered not to say anything. Even when information did start to trickle out of the agency, it was dishonest, and full of denial of any problems.

The *V*irtual Challenge

Conflicts and misunderstanding are more likely to build in a virtual world because people are not visible and they are left with assumptions. If people don't have facts and can't directly observe what's going on, they will rely on assumptions.

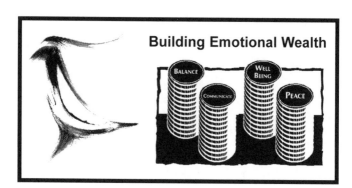

Building Emotional Wealth

BALANCE

WELL BEING

COMMUNICATE

PEACE

YOUR TURN

What can you do in your organization to support work/family balance?

How is conflict dealt with in your organization? What could be done to improve conflict resolution in your organization?

In what ways can communication in your organization be improved?

What are some other ways you could improve emotional health in your organization?

Step C.
Attend to intellectual health

- **What it means:**
  - Providing learning and developmental opportunities
- **How it works:**
  - Increase individual skills
  - Provide career development programs
  - Expose employees to emerging technologies

The Idea

Attending to intellectual health means providing learning and developmental opportunities, developing career plans, and providing state-of-the art technology. Leaders who are attentive to the intellectual needs of their employees generate intellectual capital in the organization. This intellectual capital consists of the knowledge, skills, insights and perspectives of people within the organization.

Organizations that actively promote intellectual health help individual employees and benefit as an organization from the increase in ideas and knowledge. The idea is to create a healthy partnership between the organization and its employees so that both seek ways to help the other.

Example

Canadian Imperial Bank of Commerce (CIBC) began investigating the subject of people development in the late 1980s. CIBC is striving to make the management of intellectual capital a business reality—an effort that has already changed the bank's human resources strategy and is beginning to reshape operations. At CIBC in Toronto, intellectual capital is created from the interplay of three elements:

- Individual skills needed to meet customers' needs,
- Organizational capabilities demanded by the market, and
- The strength of its franchise (customer capital).

In CIBC's model of intellectual capital formation, each of the three elements can be measured and targeted for investment. CIBC found that by helping employees develop their intellectual health, the company helped itself as well.

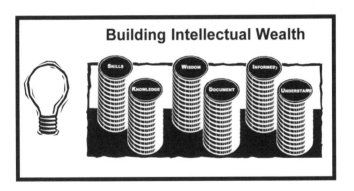

Building Intellectual Wealth

SKILLS · KNOWLEDGE · WISDOM · DOCUMENT · INFORMED · UNDERSTAND

YOUR TURN

What could you do to increase access to learning options in your organization?

How could you improve the career development programs in your organization?

How could you expose your employees to emerging technologies?

Step D.
Attend to spiritual health

- **What it means:**
  - — Building community and purpose to develop people to their full potential
- **How it works:**
  - — Bring people together
  - — Create esprit de corps
  - — Find a higher purpose
  - — Share successes

The Idea

Attending to spiritual health means building community within the organization. Just as it takes a village to raise a child, so does it take an organizational community to develop individuals to their full potential. Leaders who are attentive to the spiritual needs of their employees focus on the organizational purpose, encourage a sense of connectedness and develop an esprit de corps within teams.

Attending to spiritual health has nothing to do with religion or any set of dogmatic beliefs. Instead, spiritual health is seen as our ability to have a mission outside ourselves, to awake to the possibilities that unfold in front of us in any given moment, to experience the harmonious development of disparate individual and organizational functions, and to attempt to heal the wounds from conflict, downsizing, delayering, restructuring, etc.

Example

In the early days, the men and women of NASA had a very strong sense that their work was for a greater purpose. This was nowhere more evident than the statement heard round the world "One small step for man, one giant step for mankind." The esprit de corps among the team members was very evident in the early years. Anyone who watched a launch or landing would see employees at mission control hoop, holler and clap with excitement at their successes. The astronauts and their families were a tightly knit group, providing a sense of community and support in the best of times and worst of times.

The Virtual Challenge

Communities are normally developed when people work together and share experiences. Individuals are more likely to feel closer to the people they see everyday than the people they may work with everyday by phone, fax, E-Mail or video conferencing. Thus, in a virtual environment, building community or work spirit poses new challenges. This challenge can be addressed by sharing successes and learning experiences electronically, by deliberately getting to know each other on a community level and by spending money to bring people together.

Building Spiritual Wealth

YOUR TURN

How could you build a sense of community and connectedness in your organization?

How could you get your employees focused on a higher purpose?

What could be done to increase the sense of esprit de corps in your organization?

Where are there needs for healing in your organization?

What evidence do you see of community among your various locations? What could you do to build a sense of "virtual community" in your organization?

SKILL 5:
CREATE A LEARNING ORGANIZATION

- **Definition:** Creating the underlying values, assumptions and processes that result in high performance and competitive advantage
- **Benefits:**
  - Results in new solutions to not-yet-understood problems
  - Improves understanding of the work
  - Adds value to customers
- **Steps:**
  - A. Think systems
  - B. Seek input
  - C. Make knowledge happen
  - D. Form partnerships

Introduction

We all learn. But do we learn fast enough to survive and grow? That question is being raised more and more in board rooms across the globe. Creating a learning organization means going beyond the individual to a system that supports learning from multiple dimensions. There are a number of different perspectives regarding the nature of organizational learning. In a recent article appearing in the journal *Training and Development* (May 1994, pp. S36–47), a representative sample of leading experts in the field presented their ideas about learning. We have paraphrased their ideas.

Chris Argyris
Professor of Education and Organizational Behavior at Harvard University

Learning can be defined in two ways: detection and correction of any kind of error, or learning around routines; and double-loop learning, or learning that changes the underlying values, assumptions and programs that produced the errors in the first place. People will have to ask, "what did I do wrong here?" but they'll also have to ask, "is the way I frame reality and the way the organization frames reality in need of change?" The concept of learning has at its basis what I call productive or tough reasoning. For me that means that people make their premises explicit. And when they reach a conclusion, they craft it to be testable by logic other than their own.

Peter Block
Author and consultant

Learning and performing will become one and the same thing. Everything you say about learning will be about performance. And I don't think we will have to justify investing in it. People will get the point that learning is everything.

Rosabeth Moss Kanter
Professor of Business Administration at Harvard Business School

Learning involves not only absorbing existing information, but also creating new solutions to not-yet-understood problems. The ultimate act of learning will be embedded in the person and team as they do their work. Organizations will also want to ensure that people can learn together— that is, that they share a common vocabulary, common tools, communication channels, and commitment so they can solve problems jointly.

Ed Lawler III
Director of the Center for Effective Organizations at the School of Business Administration, University of Southern California
If organizations are going to be effective, employees have to act more like managers, and managers have to act more like employees. Managers have to understand the work better, because in many cases they will have to do more of it. For management to be a shared responsibility, employees have to understand the business and understand management skills.

Tom Peters
Author and consultant
The essential point about learning in the workplace is that the corporation is going to become a university that can add more value than its competitors around the world.

Peter Senge
Author and Director of the Center for Organizational Learning, at the Sloan School of Management, MIT
I have yet to experience any organization that comes close to exhibiting the capacities we think of when we think of learning organizations—the ability of everyone to continually challenge prevailing thinking, the ability to think systemically, and the ability to build shared visions that truly capture people's highest aspirations. Organizational learning is not the same as individual learning. New individual capabilities are a necessary condition for new organizational capabilities, but they are not sufficient to guarantee that such capabilities develop. Organization-wide learning will require critical masses of individuals operating in new ways, so that new organizational norms and habits are established. But that is not enough; it will also require new infrastructures that support learning. The only people who can by truly effective in making learning happen are managers themselves.

Noel Tichy
Author and Director of the Global Leadership
Program, University of Michigan School of Business
Administration
We live in the era of corporate revolution, driven by globalization and technological change that requires the creation of organizations without boundaries, capable of continuous radical change. Individuals will be required to creatively destroy and re-architect their organizational domains. Action learning—developing while simultaneously solving real organization problems—is the central idea that organizations must embed in their way of life.

While we cannot begin to address fully the scope of organizational learning in this section, we can outline four critical behaviors managers can do to create learning organizations:

Step A. Think systems.
Step B. Seek input.
Step C. Make knowledge happen.
Step D. Form partnerships.

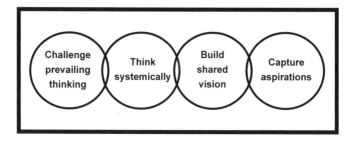

Step A.
Think systems

- **What it means:**
  - Conceptualizing all the elements of the whole, how they fit together, what functions they perform, and how the processes are orchestrated
- **How it works:**
  - Define the components
  - Define the functions
  - Define the processes
  - Understand how they become an organic system

The Idea

Seeing the organization as a system means seeing all the elements of the whole, how they fit together, what functions they perform, and how the processes are orchestrated. Doing this makes it possible to create more synergy among the integrated parts and to elevate the functions to a higher level.

In our opinion, the most comprehensive and useful models of organizational systems capture the elements of a business' components, processes and functions.

Additionally, we want to think of how technology fits into the systems and processes. This is particularly important when bringing together different managers with different and possibly overlapping capabilities. The goal is to get these managers and their respective teams to act as a single organism with interdependent parts.

Systemic thinking means thinking of organizational relationships as dynamic networks. Perceiving the organization as a network requires managers to be sensitive to the flow of information and power. Network managers encourage associates to:

- Share accurate information,
- Recognize the importance of relationships,
- Deal directly with conflict, and
- Eliminate barriers between line and staff.

Examples
NASA has a decentralized structure, where several bases around the country had different responsibilities. Johnson Space Center was in charge of managing the orbiter; Marshall Space Center was responsible for the main engines, external tank and solid rocket boosters; and Kennedy Space Center conducted launches including assembling the different components. This decentralized management created problems in maintaining communication, cooperation and accountability. Each center developed its own culture. As budget constraints began to take their toll, centers felt threatened by possible shut downs and began to view other centers as competition for scarce funds.

This set up an environment in which finger pointing became the primary response to inquiries following the Challenger tragedy. Each center had become an isolated part of the overall organization.

Ford Motor Company has been working hard to become a learning organization and see the company as interrelated systems for developing new cars. After all, people don't buy a car because it has a great suspension system. They buy a car because they like the complete package of quality, styling and function.

In the past, development engineers did not work as a system. If one team solved a problem, it usually created a problem for another team. For example a development team was trying to reduce the noise and vibration for a new Lincoln Continental. They solved their problem by adding weight to the braking system, thereby creating weight and structure problems for the braking system team.

By thinking of the company as a system, they learned that passing the problem buck did not help the company as a whole and ultimately did not serve the customer.

Thinking systemically, they brought together the brake people, development people, and chassis and suspension people. All agreed that their goal was to solve the noise and vibration problem without adding weight or cost, nor reducing quality. Once the group had agreed on the goal, they solved the problem together by revising the geometry. Once they thought systemically, they found the best solution that served the needs of the company and the customer.

YOUR
TURN

*Use the space below to create a wholistic picture of
the organizational system in NASA as described in the
example above. What are the components, the processes
and the functions?*

*What are some management behaviors that would
facilitate systems thinking in your organization?*

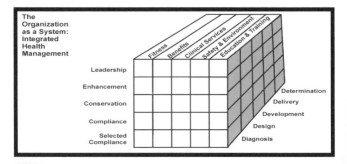

The
Organization
as a System:
Integrated
Health
Management

Fitness · Benefits · Clinical Services · Safety & Environment · Education & Training

Leadership
Enhancement
Conservation
Compliance
Selected
Compliance

Determination
Delivery
Development
Design
Diagnosis

Step B.
Seek input

- **What it means:**
  - — Being open to the outside and inside world
- **How it works:**
  - — Resist the impulse to get into turf wars
  - — Look for opportunities for cross-functional collaboration
  - — Make information accessible
  - — Hire people from whom you can learn

The Idea
Seeking multiple sources of input means being open to the outside world and the inside world. Learning requires that organizations and managers be open to a wide range of information so that they can identify challenges, threats, trends, opportunities and choices.

In a learning organization, people are not only open to new developments, but they also seek them out. With new requirements and demands constantly bombarding business leaders, it is essential to be tuned into social, political, economic, technological and customer changes.

Some companies form an issues analysis forum whose sole responsibility is to conduct external scans of changes taking place that may have an impact on the business and to share that information openly with all employees.

In order to process multiple sources of input, managers must be able to see their own values, background and experiences as not necessarily better or worse than the values, background and experiences of others (McGill et al., 1994). This pitfall of cultural superiority can even affect internal operations. For example, in traditional organizations there is normally significant conflict between engineering and marketing. Engineers and marketing specialists tend to think the organization's success revolves around their department's contribution. In learning organizations, managers resist the impulse to get into turf wars and look for opportunities for cross-functional collaboration.

Learning organizations have a commitment to knowledge that begins in the hiring process by hiring people from whom the organization can learn instead of hiring people whom the organization thinks it can teach. That commitment to learning is also demonstrated by making information accessible to everyone and by supporting efforts to seek out new information. Providing access to information resources such as the Internet promotes both learning and technology.

Leaders who are effective at seeking input ask several questions:

- What are the areas of strategic information we need to have?
- Where does that information reside?
- How do we get it?
- How do we manage it?
- How do we use it?

The implications of asking and answering these issues are multiple:

- It takes time.
- It takes resources.
- It requires someone who is responsible.
- It may require a Director of Knowledge Management.
- It requires a well-defined process.

This effort is likely to create resistance in the organization because it always requires long-term investment at the expense of short term. The leadership challenge is to make people understand that the investment has potential for great return.

Examples
Even though NASA was a research and development organization, their decline was accelerated by a lack of learning. In the years before the Challenger accident, when mechanical problems were detected, they were just corrected on the surface so that the next mission could go up. Opportunities to reassess the underlying causes and assumptions creating the problem were bypassed.

Additionally, the leadership of NASA had become too closely connected with the contractor industry. Top executives moved back and forth between contractor organizations and the agency. This inhibited fresh ideas or viewpoints from the outside.

With increasing pressure to maintain an unrealistic flight schedule, the management did not seek out information from anyone who might have an opinion other than their own. Anything that might have caused them to stop what they were doing, look and learn was discouraged.

It was even reported that officials at Marshall Space Flight Center had shredded weekly reports on problems with the solid rocket boosters.

Ingersol Rand, an Industrial Grinding Tool Manufacturer, was able to turn lagging sales into a marketplace winner by injecting learning and multi-functional teams into their product development process. Engineers teamed up with marketing personnel to travel into the field. The engineers met with customers to learn about how people used products.

At location after location they noticed their tools wrapped with layers of duct tape. Asked why the duct tape, customers consistently responded that there was no comfortable handle to grip when operating the machine. The duct tape was a home-made solution to product design not tailored to meet customer needs. The engineers went back to the drawing board to redesign the product, incorporating a comfortable grip ergonomically designed to the way the tool was used. It became a run-away best selling product for the company and a leader in the market.

YOUR TURN

What information is most strategically important to us?

How could we be more effective in seeking out information from external sources?

How could we be more effective in seeking out and sharing information from internal sources?

How can we demonstrate our commitment to knowledge?

Step C.
Make knowledge happen

- **What it means:**
  - — Continually generating new knowledge and encouraging entrepreneurial behavior based on that knowledge
- **How it works:**
  - — Suspend control
  - — Provide more flexibility
  - — Transform collective intelligence into a source of competitive advantage

The Idea

Making knowledge happen means using the information that people have access to in mission critical ways. The idea is to create more customer focus so that employees on the front line can get a better sense of changing relationships and demands from their customers. Making knowledge happen also involves encouraging entrepreneurial behavior and giving more flexibility to associates.

Many organizations change to more of a network or cluster structure in order to facilitate collaboration both internally and externally. The outcome of these changes is that the organization generates new knowledge continually. This knowledge needs to be shared throughout the organization so that collective intelligence becomes a source of competitive advantage.

In order to create a learning organization, managers must suspend their need for control. Delayering and restructuring efforts have created flatter organizations with less hierarchical controls, but the structural shifts must be accompanied by managerial mental shifts if they are going to work.

Workgroup technologies can enable this step. These technologies can make the use of knowledge possible, but without adequate processes and leadership, the technologies alone will not produce the desired results. Technology is a necessary, but not sufficient, condition for making knowledge happen.

Examples
Nordstrom Department Store employees on the front line have access to all resources within the company to help them solve customer problems. They can communicate to warehouse personnel, customer service, and the buying department to gain information necessary to solve a problem. In addition, they are given the authority to fix the problem without checking with a supervisor.

This strategy is paying off for Nordstroms. Traditional department stores have been in financial distress for the past decade, but in each new market that Nordstroms enters, they beat the competition. Their success is not from selling anything different from their competition, or from selling it cheaper. The difference is customer service, and the customers are voting with their checkbooks and charge cards.

Nordstroms also promotes open communication between employees, customer service and buying departments so that customer-derived information about problem products goes directly to the department responsible for the buying. In this way, with a direct line of communication from the customer, Nordstroms can be more responsive to changes in customer needs.

In the extremely cost competitive world of electronics, where cutting costs is critical to survival and growth, Motorola has benefited from its commitment to learning. Spending more than $100 million a year (4 percent of payroll) on training and education, Motorola has invested in learning and gotten the payback through reduced costs. Since 1987, Motorola has cut costs by $3 billion, without downsizing or massive restructuring. Motorola believes that for every $1 spent on education, it gets a return of $3 in product sales.

YOUR TURN

How can you make collective intelligence a source of competitive advantage and/or for real time, mission critical applications?

How could you provide more flexibility in your organization?

How could you suspend control in your organization?

In what ways could you free initiative?

Step D.
Form partnerships

- **What it means:**
  - Selecting partners who can teach
- **How it works:**
  - Look beyond the organizational boundaries
  - Develop strategic alliances
  - Establish guidelines
  - Align partnerships with organizational vision, strategy and goals

The Idea

Creating a learning organization extends beyond the bounds of our own organizations. We can learn from partners as well. Just as organizations need to hire people from whom they can learn, they could also select partners who have the ability to teach them as well.

Same time/different place/different time workgroup technologies have eliminated boundaries that once constrained the forming of partnerships. Individuals within multiple departments, organizations and geographic locations can work together in tandem to improve the delivery capacity as well as learning capacity.

Example

In 1992, Lotus was at a significant disadvantage to Microsoft on scale issues. Lotus could not possibly compete with Microsoft by throwing resources at key issues and opportunities. Microsoft had much deeper pockets and more feet on the street.

An alternative way for Lotus to compete was to establish strategic alliances with partners. By the end of 1992 Lotus' business partners program was fragmented, inconsistent and weak. The revenue contribution from partners was less than 5 percent, while mutual commitment and satisfaction ratings were low.

To correct this situation Lotus created a partnering strategy that aimed at winning in the marketplace and gaining a competitive advantage. This strategy provided partners with an opportunity to enhance their image, increase sales and enhance opportunities for new markets and businesses.

The strategic alliances led to greater credibility, marketing knowledge, and sales teaming for large scale solution sales. By the end of 1994, Lotus had established partnerships with major players, such as IBM, HP, Sun, Compaq, Apple, AT&T, EDS, Andersen Consulting, Novell, SAP, and Big 6 accounting firms. In strictly quantitative terms, Lotus had increased its strategic alliances from 2,000 to 8,000. By 1995, Lotus had established a competitive partnering position to Microsoft. The outcomes of the partnering strategy were:

- Notes was established as the workgroup standard.
- Lotus was rated a top ten "partnering company" in a survey of over 200 companies.
- Business executives worldwide know Notes.
- Lotus developed substantial capacity worldwide for selling, supporting, and training.
- Notes seats increased from 300K to 3M.
- Lotus' reputation improved as a partner.

How did Lotus accomplish this task? It started with a comprehensive strategy, recruited the best possible people, built high performing teams, established guidelines, communicated widely, upgraded skills and thought outside the box.

When the business partner strategy was launched, Jim Manzi said, "It is essential that we develop the ability to build mutually rewarding partnerships with companies of scale who share our vision of both the business and the competitive environment."

Finally, Lotus insisted that the partnering strategy be consistent with key partnering principles:

- Identify compelling Lotus and partner objectives
- Partner proactively with the best companies
- Know the partners' strategy, organization and concerns
- Pick key people to make the partnership succeed
- Construct flexible, win-win agreements
- Communicate openly, honestly and directly
- Involve the "deliverers" from the beginning
- Meet commitments
- Define, measure and promote success
- Expand to new areas of mutual benefit

While the partnering strategy significantly increased Lotus' capacity to compete, it missed a critical opportunity to learn more systematically from its partners. If Lotus had created a mechanism to learn from every transaction and to translate that information into competitive advantage, it may have improved its competitive position against Microsoft and Internet providers.

YOUR TURN

How can you create partnering strategies to increase your capacity to deliver value to customers?

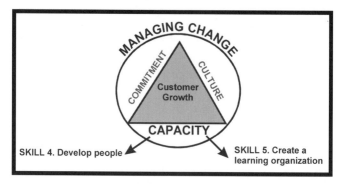

Task II. Capacity Exercise

In our task to build capacity, we have discussed two skills:

- Develop people
- Create a learning organization

Please review these two skills and decide what actions you can take in your organization to build capacity.

Knowledge
Skills
+ Capacity

Solution

Task II. Building Capacity Summary

Human capacity involves providing people with the knowledge, skill and capability to be solution-oriented agents for the customer. People development is built by attending to the physical, intellectual, emotional and spiritual needs of employees. High performing teams require high levels of employee job satisfaction and commitment, which is the result of empowering people and providing challenge and an appropriate amount of stress. In a virtual environment, when you don't see people all the time, these skills are more easily overlooked, but they are no less important.

The second part of building capacity involves creating a learning organization. In a learning organization, all departments and functions within the organization are viewed as part of an interdependent system. Each division can learn from each other or from outside partnerships. Employees are given the knowledge, the authority and the autonomy to solve customer problems. In this way the organization is gaining information directly from the customer and is able to respond immediately to customer needs. In a learning organization, leaders take time to debrief successful and unsuccessful projects. They take time to learn from victories and from mistakes or disasters.

Finally, the learning organization is in tune with the strategic information it needs to be successful, and it has processes and leadership in place to build, maintain and use it.

Task III.
Aligning the Culture

Key Ingredients:
- Norms, values, rituals and assumptions
- The organizational unconscious

Critical Skills:
6. Articulate the cultural requirements for success
7. Create a cultural revolution

Managing corporate culture change has emerged as a top priority for most business leaders. Cultural norms, values and rituals are being increasingly recognized as the key factors that either enhance or retard change and renewal initiatives. Indeed, if corporate culture is not compatible with business strategies, hopes for success and growth are dim.

For many leaders, corporate culture change seems so esoteric and "soft" that deciding to shape it, manage it or change it seems overwhelming. This section will help to demystify the notion of corporate culture change.

Anthropologists and other social scientists have long studied the dynamics of culture in the everyday lives of people. As readers of *National Geographic* and viewers of international news reports, we have been fascinated, sometimes perplexed, and occasionally horrified by the vast array of customs, traditions, world views and norms that define the different human cultures around the globe.

Strangely, the power of culture in our own lives has gone largely unexamined. As if by magic, we accept our own cultural ways as a given. The culture has become our organizational unconscious. "It's just the way we do things around here."

We are largely unaware of the specific norms and values that influence our lives. And we underestimate the power of the culture to affect us routinely and profoundly. Fortunately, we do have the ability to create norms of our own choosing.

Those working with corporate culture believe that people can and should play an active role in choosing the cultural environment in which they work. In this section, you will learn two skills for aligning the culture:

Skill 6. Articulate the cultural requirements for success

Skill 7. Create a cultural revolution

The **V**irtual Challenge

Aligning the culture is particularly important in the virtual world because distance and diversity have changed many of the rules, assumptions and values that have guided our behaviors in traditional organizations around the globe. Trying to conduct global business when there are differences in language, time zones, and technologies poses new cultural challenges for the 21st-century leader. On the most basic level, independent of the national context, organizational cultures influence how people act as individuals in their particular setting. The first step of cultural alignment in the virtual world is to establish the norms and values that inform how teams need to act in a global context.

SKILL 6:
ARTICULATE THE CULTURAL REQUIREMENTS FOR SUCCESS

- **Definition:** Identifying the values, behaviors and attitudes necessary to achieve desired results
- **Benefits:**
  — Increases the chances for strategic success
  — Communicates what is important
- **Steps:**
  A. Review stated values and operating principles
  B. Translate values and principles into norms and behaviors

Introduction
In a recent study of best practices in corporate restructuring, 43 percent of senior executives identified a dysfunctional culture as a major barrier to success (Wyatt, 1993). Apparently, executives are finding that no matter how much effort they invest in crafting the right strategy, structure and systems, their efforts do not achieve the desired results unless the culture is aligned with the strategy. Dr. Gwen Stern, a cultural anthropologist at Wyatt, believes the key to changing behaviors and attitudes is for "leadership to define the new values of the culture and why cultural change must happen. Then, leadership must act quickly and decisively to show they mean it."

There are several key characteristics that are common in a "renewing culture." Since seven seems to be a magical number these days, we present the seven factors of highly effective cultures.

111

**The Seven Characteristics
of Highly Effective Cultures**

1. There is a common cause shared by all levels of the organization.

2. People think and act "outside the box." Doing things the "same old way" is no longer rewarded.

3. There is a healthy tension between stability and agility.

4. People learn from mistakes—there is more emphasis on fixing the problem than assigning the blame.

5. Communication is direct and honest and flows in all directions.

6. Information is shared openly.

7. Leaders support flexibility.

Even though these characteristics may be common in effective changing corporate culture efforts, leaders must articulate the characteristics of cultural success within their own organization. To do this, start with a clear understanding of the strategy, structure and systems and then ask, "What are the values and norms we will need to implant and have operating in our culture to make it possible for our strategy, structure and systems to work?" and "Does the virtual environment pose any demands that require a different set of norms and values?"

To articulate the cultural requirements for success in your organization, you will be taking two steps:

Step A. Review stated values and operating principles.
Step B. Translate them into norms and behaviors.

Step A.
Review stated values and operating principles

- **What it means:**
  - — Considering the enduring elements of the old culture and preserving what still works
- **How it works:**
  - — Review vision and value statements
  - — Identify those values and principles that are still congruent with the strategy

The Idea

Most organizations have vision and value statements written on posters adorning the walls. In Skill 1, Step A, you listed the core values that guide your organizational behavior. Think about the values that are currently hanging on the office walls in your company. Management hopes that these posters will remind employees of the values and vision of the organization and result in cultural alignment. But questions remain:

- Do these statements and posters reflect how things really work in the organizational culture?
- Do the statements capture the essential character of the organization?
- Are the statements currently consistent with the strategy, structure, systems and leadership behavior?

In an effective changing corporate culture effort, it is just as important to maintain the values that still reflect your deepest aspirations as a company, as it is to articulate new values that reflect how you need to operate in a virtual world. Leaders need to consider what enduring elements of the old culture it wants to preserve and what needs to be changed. Again, there has to be a healthy balance between stability and change.

Example

As NASA renews its organization by reviewing the stated values and operating principles, it will find that many of the things they were doing worked. In the early days, quality as it related to safety was a major priority. It would be helpful to NASA to reevaluate how things worked back then. Perhaps interviewing associates involved on projects in the early days could provide some insight. Clearly, not everything that NASA was doing was destructive. They had successfully created a positive public image. In fact, they had one of the best images of any governmental agency and succeeded in making each flight a media event. Although the Challenger tragedy shook the public trust for a time, reassessing NASA's culture to determine if it still fits with their current focus will be an important step to recovery.

**YOUR
TURN**

*Review your vision statements, values, operating
principles or any other documents that describe how
you want your organization to run. List those values,
norms and principles you want to preserve.*

*Compare this new list of norms and values with the
original company value statement. What are the major
differences? How do you feel about those changes?*

Step B.
Translate values and principles into norms and behaviors

- **What it means:**
  — Anchoring values with concrete examples
- **How it works:**
  — Choose 10 values that describe the essential character of your desired organization
  — Operationalize those values with 3 to 5 norm statements

The Idea

Every value needs several norms to anchor it in reality. Without these normative anchors, it is impossible to implant the values or put the aspirations of your culture into action. For example, we may say we value respect, but what does that mean? Everyone may have a different image of what "respect" looks like or how it exists in day-to-day operations. Therefore, it is important to ground each value in a set of illustrative behaviors or norms that make it clear what we would expect to see in attitudes and behaviors if the value really existed in the culture. Lets take the value "respect." We can translate respect into the following set of behaviors and norms:

Around here we:
- Value different perspectives;
- Think inclusively;
- Treat individuals as whole persons with unique needs;
- Promote understanding;
- Seek to eliminate bias;
- Consider the points of view of all groups.

We can translate the value "sharing information" into the following behaviors and norms:

Around here we:
- Are open and honest;
- Give people information in a timely manner;
- Consistently use group enabling technology;
- Provide proper training in the use of technology;
- Stay current with emerging technologies that enable information sharing;
- Reward information sharing.

There is great power in this step. Organizations can create norms of their own choosing if they involve people in the process and specify exactly the norms and behaviors that are expected.

Example
A company using workgroup technologies might want to translate the value "sensitivity to cultural differences" when working in a virtual world.

Around here we:
- Are open minded;
- Build in opportunities for face-to-face communications;
- Interact in social ways;
- Are sensitive to language differences by using visuals whenever possible;
- Use short, to-the-point sentences;
- Develop norms around cultural differences;
- Strive for equity of time convenience;
- Are sensitive to issues that are best presented in primary language.

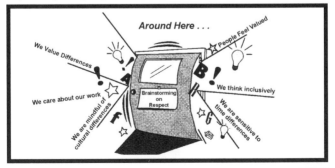

YOUR TURN

Choose 5 to 10 values you believe need to be implanted in your organization's culture. These should be the essential characteristics that you want to define your organization's reputation and that support your strategy, structure and vision. Then, translate each value into 3 to 5 norm statements. This will help you measure how well each value has been activated into your culture.

SKILL 7:
CREATE A CULTURAL REVOLUTION

- **Definition:** Making the business shift to a global environment in which technology-enabled, virtual teams are requirements for success

- **Benefits:**
    - Shocks the organization—avoids "boiling frog" syndrome
    - Aligns the values with the strategy—from words to actions

- **Steps:**
    - A. Diagnose your current culture
    - B. Develop programs
    - C. Deliver skills and support
    - D. Determine progress

Introduction

While Skill 6 gets you beyond the poster on the wall (values are aligned and norms are specific), it does not achieve radical cultural change. "Changing corporate culture" is a polite way of saying "radical revolution." As shocking as that statement sounds, it may be necessary, given the changes imposed upon us by the shift to a global environment in which technology-enabled virtual teams are now requirements for survival and success.

To achieve this revolution in a relatively painless and peaceful way, a sound process is required. One such process is the 4D model developed by Possibilities, Inc. This model suggests a systematic approach to change that guides the organization through the phases of the four Ds: Diagnosis, Develop, Delivery and Determination.

There are four steps for cultural revolution:

Step A. Diagnose your current culture.
Step B. Develop programs.
Step C. Deliver skills and support.
Step D: Determine progress.

Step A.
Diagnose your current culture

- **What it means:**
  - Collecting statistically significant data
- **How it works:**
  - Select the sample
  - Decide on means of administration, e.g., electronic, or paper and pencil
  - Attach a cover letter
  - Decide on incentives
  - Follow up with non-respondents

The Idea

In Skill 6 you learned a template for designing a culture audit for your organization, and you identified some norms and values you would want to assess in your culture.

As you develop your own survey, remember that technology-enabled virtual work requires different norms and values than traditional work. Make sure your survey does not reinforce individualism. Also, think about specific ways to encourage virtuality and teamwork in your culture. Once you have decided what you want to measure, you will need to decide how you are going to measure it. Here are a few steps and tips for conducting a cultural survey in your organization.

1. **Who.** Decide if you want to administer the survey to all associates or a random sample. There is an educational advantage to sending everyone the survey because it contains messages about the desired norms and values in the new culture.

2. **How.** Decide how to administer the survey, i.e., via the web, paper and pencil, distributed through management.

3. **Boost response.** Here are several techniques to boost survey response:

   - Have the CEO include a cover letter with the survey explaining its purpose and what will be done with the results.
   - Have associates do the survey on company time.
   - Set up a lottery or sweepstakes reward for all people who complete the survey.
   - Include a token reward with the survey, such as a coupon, lottery ticket or dollar bill.

4. **Create safety.** Protecting confidentiality will help people feel safe enough to be honest. Simply include a control card with the survey. Have people send the survey to a third party and send the control card to your staff. Follow up with non-respondents by offering a smaller, but different type of incentive.

With incentives, company time and follow-up, response rates can exceed 70 percent. Without follow-up, incentives or the option of completing the survey on company time, you can expect response rates between 20 and 25 percent.

Analyze the Results
Results can be analyzed either internally or through an outside contractor. The analysis should summarize the strengths (i.e., those norms that were rated as very important—4.0 on a 5-point scale—as well as true—3.0 on a 5-point scale). It should also identify the weakness in the organizational culture (i.e., those norms that were rated below 2.5 on the agreement scale). Further, the survey should analyze incongruities (i.e., those norms that

had large gaps between the importance ratings and the strength ratings). Specifically, it is possible to identify gaps as follows:

> 2.0 = danger

1.5–2.0 = problem

1.0–1.5 = concern

The analysis should also provide a directional indication— which norms are getting better and which norms are getting worse. If you would like to administer and analyze your culture audit on-line, go to www.THINQ.com. THINQ has a web-based tool that will make your diagnosis easy.

Communicate the Results
The most important part of any survey process is what happens with the results once you have them. At a minimum, the results need to be summarized and distributed to the people who participated in the survey.

Ideally, focus groups should be conducted—based on the survey results—to probe more deeply into those areas of concern. The facilitator of those focus groups should ask participants to describe the problem, e.g., poor communications or lack of involvement, fairness, trust or respect. Then, the group should do a Pareto analysis to determine root causes of the problems.

Finally, the group should generate some specific ideas that would be easy to implement, practical and cost-effective. The ideas generated from these focus groups usually contain some easy-to-implement, low-cost ideas ("low hanging fruit") that show visible evidence of the leadership's commitment to change. These should be identified and implemented as soon as possible.

Technology can be used to post the information and provide open on-line discussion groups.

Example
Here are two sets of norms that many virtual organizations include in their surveys:

Collaboration:
We have deeply spirited, generative conversations.

We feel heard.

We share what we think and feel.

We have shared goals and mental models.

We look for ways to create and inspire vs. command and control.

We don't engage in defensive routines.

We realize that we can't meet the challenges we face independently in isolation.

We use technology to accelerate learning.

Communications:
We seek first to understand.
We communicate with each other as whole people who are connected and trusting.
We feel understood and involved no matter where we are in the world.
We are sensitive to differences in time zones.
We look for ways to close the distance between us.
We leverage diversity.
We make good decisions about how to communicate on various issues, e.g., face-to-face, E-Mail, etc.

The Virtual Challenge

Developing a survey strategy in a virtual environment creates unique challenges. Questions to assess norms and values will be different in a virtual environment than in a single setting. Because associates may be working in different environments, different cultures and even different countries, these differences need to be taken into consideration when developing the survey. Perhaps you will need different surveys for different languages.

In a virtual world, company time and personal time become more blurred, so other types of incentives need to be strengthened to increase response.

YOUR TURN

In the space below, outline the steps you are going to take to diagnose your culture. After you decide what you are going to measure, you may want to revisit your strategy to identify compatibilities, incompatibilities and possible ways to revamp your strategy or your survey. In this process, make sure you are identifying specific ways to encourage virtuality and teamwork. When you are done, ask yourself, "Do these norms and values reflect a radical shift in the way we do business in a technology-enabled, virtual world, or are they just an incremental alteration of the same old way?"

Step B.
Develop programs

- **What it means:**
  - Creating the resources required for success
- **How it works:**
  - Identify and train role models and champions
    - Just-in-time training
  - Communicate learning from the diagnosis
  - Involve people in the transformation process

The Idea
In this step, the emphasis is on developing the programs
required for success. Effective and lasting change requires
a broad base of leadership skills and support within the
organization. Internal resources need to be trained as
role models and exemplars for desired changes. It is also
important during this phase to communicate what was
learned from the cultural diagnosis process and explain
the effects of the culture on organizational behavior, personal performance, virtual work, and business objectives.
The key objective is to involve people at all levels and all
locations in the change effort. Workgroup technologies
can greatly accelerate learning and involvement in this
process. The specific desired results are internal productivity and profitability as well as customer productivity
and profitability.

The *V*irtual Challenge

In today's global economy, organizational development needs to incorporate "distance learning" for diverse populations. Given the fact that work teams now operate at different times and different places for shorter periods of time, it is no longer as viable to develop people through traditional, classroom instruction.

   Time-consuming training programs in a single location are less attractive. Training needs to be on demand and be delivered anytime, anywhere. We need to explore alternative delivery mechanisms for "just-in-time learning." Technology can be used to allow employees to access modular training materials wherever they are, tailored to their individual needs, and with instant progress feedback. Similarly, we need to develop programs that are sensitive to the diverse needs of global teams.

Developmental Challenges

Competition   Compensation   Culture

YOUR TURN

What are the particular development challenges you face given the issues of distance and diversity in your organization?

Step C.
Deliver skills and support

- **What it means:**
  — Implementing programs for mission-critical changes
- **How it works:**
  — Equip people with skills
    • Distance learning
    • CBT
    • Classroom
  — Create a supportive environment

The Idea
The key concept in this step is to deliver the ideas and goals of the diagnosis and development phases (Steps A and B) through a multi-faceted intervention, using a variety of workgroup technologies. Leadership provides the vision and commitment that drive the whole change effort. During this phase, the primary job of management is to help interpret, communicate and reinforce the organizational mission by supporting collaboration, communications and teamwork.

Delivery is a two-pronged approach emphasizing skills and support. Distance learning programs are designed to equip people with the skills they need to achieve their goals even when located in remote areas. At the same time, the organization and work teams must provide a supportive environment for the acquisition and application of new skills—even though some technologies and skills may represent a radical shift in the way work gets done. Leaders need to design systems to reward the required norms in the new culture.

Example

One company, Company A, trained its service employees by having them work temporarily at a company that provided better service, Company B. Cash managers were allowed to work in the cash management department to learn from the best. Reciprocally, the production employees from Company B were allowed to work in Company A's production department to learn from them. By working collaboratively, both companies benefited by learning from the other's expertise in a particular area.

Year: 1980
    Help wanted
Key Punch Operator.
Excellent typing
skills required.

Year: 2010
    Help wanted
Network Guru. Able
to work with other
people in virtual
teams.

YOUR
TURN

What new skills will your team need to function effectively in the new culture?

How will your efforts to support these changes need to change in a virtual world?

Step D.
Determine progress

- **What it means:**
    — Evaluating results and recycling the process
- **How it works:**
    — Assess how far the organization has come
    — Learn from successes and failures
    — Incorporate learnings into renewal efforts

The Idea

In this step, the goals are to determine the results of the culture change efforts and to recycle the process. Since change is a never-ending process, this step is both the end and the beginning of the 4D process. Leaders need to take a hard look at how far the organization has come and how far it still needs to go—and then rekindle the desire to proceed. This step provides the systematic follow-up that is crucial to lasting change.

Leaders will need to:

- Create a consistency of purpose;
- Adopt a philosophy congruent with the age we live in; and
- Make change a well-orchestrated process, rather than a series of isolated events.

In determining progress, it is particularly valuable to use workgroup technologies to learn from our successes and our setbacks. We can debrief electronically in order to capture the learnings from our intervention and incorporate those learnings in our on-going renewal efforts.

Example

On the brink of impending doom in 1983, the Harley-Davidson Motor Company made a phenomenal comeback, in part as a result of becoming a learning organization. The company wanted to not only learn from mistakes, but also understand the underlying causes of mistakes and successes.

For example, at a strategic planning meeting, the management was trying to solve a production and capacity problem. They hadn't been able to manufacture at a level to meet demand. The management was trying to decide whether to build another manufacturing plant. Since the company had embraced the learning organization philosophy, the management group now discussed the issue in a new way. By looking at the impact on people, capital and quality and questioning underlying assumptions, the team came to understand that they didn't need to build another plant. They needed to use an existing plant in a different way.

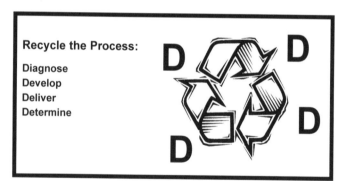

Recycle the Process:

Diagnose
Develop
Deliver
Determine

YOUR TURN

How well does your organization learn from previous interventions?

What are the special challenges and opportunities for learning in a technology-enabled virtual world?

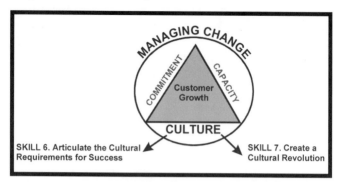

SKILL 6. Articulate the Cultural Requirements for Success

SKILL 7. Create a Cultural Revolution

Task III. Alignment Exercise

In this task to Align the Culture, you learned two skills:

- Articulate the cultural requirements for success
- Create a cultural revolution

Please review Skills 6 and 7, then decide what three actions you can take to align the culture in your organization.

Task III. Aligning the Culture Summary

When the corporate culture is not aligned with the goals and strategies of an organization working toward renewal efforts, frustration is the likely outcome. The corporate cultures of organizations have a powerful influence over how things get done. Ideally, we want to be sure that our values and operating principles translate correctly into the norms and behaviors of day-to-day life on the job. These norms and values need to reflect what is necessary in technology-enabled virtual environments. Therefore, we need to consider new ways of dealing with distance and diversity and new ways of collaborating, communicating and teaming.

To ensure that the norms and behaviors of the organization are in alignment with the new vision and values of the renewal effort, a radical change in the culture may be required. This change requires a systems approach such as the 4D process (Diagnosis, Develop, Delivery, and Determination). Leaders who want to align their culture not only need to articulate the cultural requirements for success, but they also need to create a cultural revolution to have any hopes of achieving them. This revolution imposes new demands on leaders. In addition to Management By Walking Around (MBWA), the virtual leader has to Lead by Flying Around (LBFA) and Lead by Surfing Around (LBSA). These new leadership requirements mean new skills and abilities for the already-buffeted corporate executive. And, to add insult to injury, virtual executives will need to invite 360-degree feedback from their global constituents that will expose their strengths and weaknesses on the cultural variables required for success in the virtual world. In the companies that are engaging in changing corporate culture efforts in

order to compete in this global whitewater, the surviving managers are finding that the "old ways of doing things" are largely obsolete. In the scramble to stay competitive and to meet these new challenges, the skills in this book will help leaders navigate the blind corners and forked roads they face on a daily basis.

Remember, there are three simple principles in culture change:

1. Engage people in a meaningful dialogue about the culture they want and need to succeed.

2. Build core values into everything.

3. Measure progress.

Task IV.
Managing Change

Key Ingredients:
- Dealing with the fact that things are not, and may never be, what they were

Critical Skills:
8. Promote understanding
9. Facilitate acceptance of what cannot be changed
10. Enable change

Introduction

In the first three tasks of this book—Maximizing Commitment, Building Capacity and Aligning the Culture—you have explored and understood many changes you will need to make in order to renew your organization and compete successfully in a global economy. To the extent that you implement the action plans you have developed for your organizations, these changes will have significant implications for you and for the people in your organization. In this last task on changing corporate culture, you will learn the skills you need to help yourself and your people manage these cultural and skill changes successfully.

Several of the most consequential changes introduced in this book relate to the demands of moving to technology-enabled virtual work and/or e-commerce. In a virtual world, there are different rules, different assumptions and different values. People are also faced with the need to navigate the global workplace in which there are different times, different languages and different technologies. These differences require changes in habits, patterns and ways of managing time. In this world, a person may be obliged to function on multiple teams with fewer face-to-face meetings. And they must learn to communicate effectively in electronic meetings by using PC technology.

Generally, there are two types of change: unexpected change and expected change.

Unexpected change occurs and causes us to react. On a personal level it might be a sudden job loss or a natural disaster. When a significant event occurs, you can either manage the change and become healthier as a result, or you can choose not to manage the change, thereby increasing the chance of unhappiness and even illness.

On the corporate level, this type of change might be the loss of a key player on a virtual team or a glitch in the technology that slows down a project. How we and our organization react to unplanned changes makes a big difference in whether the change provides opportunity for growth or derails us.

Anticipated changes are those that we undergo intentionally. On a personal level it might mean accepting a new job offer, getting married or moving to a new city. In the virtual world it might be bringing about change in corporate culture, developing a new virtual team or adopting new technologies.

Everyone is Affected
Whether unexpected or anticipated, change affects everyone at every level of an organization. Change can have both a positive and negative impact on employees. It may be perceived differently by different people, in different places and in different cultures. Even positive events demand skills to manage change. In a simple sense, change means that things are not, and may never be, what they once were. Change involves a disruption of existing activities and feelings and requires learning new ways of doing things.

Resistance is a common human reaction to change. In today's changing environment it is imperative that managers understand not only how to create change in their organizations but also how to manage the human change process in a virtual world.

Managing change is letting go of illusions, accepting reality and focusing on new possibilities. Change requires working out new agreements and finding tools to move beyond the current status.

Three Phases of Change

Managing change involves three different processes: understanding, accepting, and changing. A healthy response to change includes understanding what has happened; accepting what can't be changed; and changing what we can, to achieve a new level of health. Often the barriers to healthy change include resistance, denial and repression. These processes can lead to negative thoughts, negative emotions, destructive behavior, stagnation and even physical illness. Building resiliency to change leads people to be more positive and accepting of the change process.

Healthy response to change includes understanding, accepting, changing and moving forward. Managing change in a positive way results in improved health.

Barriers to healthy change include resistance, denial and repression. These can lead to negative thoughts, negative emotions, destructive behavior and even physical illness.

In this task you will work on three skills:

Skill 8. Promote Understanding

Skill 9. Facilitate Acceptance of What Cannot Be Changed

Skill 10. Enable Change

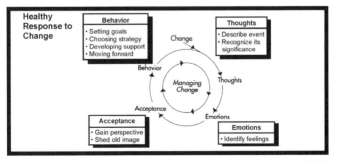

Change Assessment

Before you begin, please take a few moments to complete this questionnaire. It's important for you to understand where your department or organization is on the continuum of change. Do not spend too much time on each item. Respond how you honestly feel, not how you think you should respond.

In the space below, briefly describe a change your organization or department is experiencing.

In response to each of the following statements, write down the number that corresponds most closely to what you believe the people in your department or organization are feeling about the change.

0 = Disagree   2 = Agree
1 = Somewhat Agree   3 = Strongly Agree

_____ 1. People don't agree with this change and resent having to go through it.

_____ 2. People believe that the change makes sense and will benefit everyone.

_____ 3. People are excited about the change and have a vision of a better future.

_____ 4. The staff doesn't appear to feel anything about the change.

_____ 5. People have both positive and negative feelings about the change.

_____ 6. This change allows me to feel good about myself.

_____ 7. This whole thing will blow over soon if we just wait it out.

_____ 8. The staff knows what they can do to make things work.

_____ 9. In general, people are pleased with the steps the organization is taking to make this change a success.

_____ 10. People feel that nothing good will come from this change.

_____ 11. The change can be beneficial if everyone pitches in to make it work.

_____ 12. The change has already proven to be beneficial and positive.

_____ 13. Employees are upset about how this has been carried out.

_____ 14. Things are not what they could be, but it's starting to make sense.

_____ 15. Everyone is working together to make this a success.

_____ 16. Peoples' enthusiasm and enjoyment in work are at an all-time low.

_____ 17. People feel good about what they're learning and doing.

_____ 18. What we are doing now is better than the old way.

_____ 19. This change will affect others more than it will affect me.

_____ 20. The worst is over and the best is yet to come.

_____ 21. I feel like people have more energy and enthusiasm since we started making changes.

Score Your Change Assessment

To score your Change Assessment, simply transfer your
numbers from the previous page to the corresponding
lines below. Then add the numbers in each column. Write
your column totals in the screened boxes at the bottom of
each column. Note that the numbers go across the three
columns, from left to right.

1. _____	2. _____	3. _____
4. _____	5. _____	6. _____
7. _____	8. _____	9. _____
10. _____	11. _____	12. _____
13. _____	14. _____	15. _____
16. _____	17. _____	18. _____
19. _____	20. _____	21. _____
A	B	C
Resistance	Acceptance	Commitment to Change

Your Phase of Change

The three scores from your Change Assessment represent different phases of change. The highest score is an indication of where your department or organization is today on the continuum of change. Where they are on the continuum of change is influenced by many factors that we will explore in the rest of this book.

SKILL 8:
PROMOTE UNDERSTANDING

- **Definition:** Promoting understanding of changes by providing information and facilitating open communication
- **Benefits:**
  — Allows employees to comprehend their situation and express how they feel
- **Steps:**
  A. Describe the event
  B. Identify feelings and beliefs

Change of any kind requires a certain amount of sacrifice and the experience of loss. Resistance can be a temporary and natural part of change, or it can be prolonged and disruptive. A person's first response to change may be the tendency to ignore the event, suppress feelings or underestimate its significance. It's important for managers to promote understanding of the changes taking place by providing adequate information about the changes through open and honest communication. It is also important that employees be allowed to understand and express how they feel about the changes.

You can promote understanding by using the following two steps:

Step A. Describe the event.
Step B. Identify feelings and beliefs.

Step A.
Describe the event

- **What it means:**
  - Understanding the type and significance of change
- **How it works:**
  - Explore the significance
  - Understand the demands

Describing the event includes the ability to understand the type of event that has occurred, the significance of the event and the demands created by it.

Events can be unexpected or expected, positive or negative. There are many types of unexpected events such as job loss, job transfer or an equipment malfunction.

Expected events may include accepting a new job offer, opening a new division, introducing new computer systems or planning stages of corporate culture change.

Recognizing the significance of the event involves exploring what the event means to people. Taking the time to focus on the event and experience its significance is an important step in managing change in a positive way.

During periods of change it is essential for managers to do what they can to create an environment of trust. The best way to promote trust is for people to believe that they have all the information. People going through change will have a tremendous thirst for information. They need to fully understand what is happening to them and to believe they know everything. Vagueness feeds anxiety, which feeds fear, which causes paralysis and resistance. When people don't feel they have all the information, they tend to speculate on the information that's missing—this can become a great breeding ground for the destructive rumor mill.

Use workgroup technology to allow access to information and give people a sense of control over the information. Create bulletin boards of information about every aspect of the changes happening at all levels of the organization and let people access the information at their own pace. This is particularly important for virtual teams where feelings of isolation from what's going on is natural. Open communication and free-flowing, accessible information can go a long way to helping people feel that the organization is keeping them informed. It might be a good time to start a newsletter to help keep people up to date.

Soon after the change event occurs, people usually experience the demands created by the event. These demands may include learning new skills, finding support or letting go of old beliefs or ways of doing things.

Managers should help each employee understand the ramifications of the changes and what it will demand of them. Once these demands are defined, it is essential to provide the training and support necessary to meet the demands. Education, new equipment or tools to help people implement the changes will help them feel empowered and committed to the change. Providing support creates a positive outlook among employees. They can start to feel that there is something good in it for them.

Different groups within the organization will have different levels of demands placed on them from the change. There is often a direct relationship between the level of impact and the level of resistance encountered. A useful tool for analyzing the levels of support needed and the impact of the change process is the Stakeholder Analysis (see bottom of this page).

By looking at the key players and the relationship between demands and level of support, managers can determine where intervention activities may need to focus. Some groups may require more effort, information and resources than others during the change process to ensure success.

Example
A dramatic example of an unexpected, negative event involves the horrible story of a burning platform on an off-shore oil rig. Employees working on the platforms in the raging, Arctic Sea were instructed never to jump off the platform in an emergency. Tragically one evening, an uncontrollable fire broke out on the platform. All of the men were killed, with the exception of one worker who jumped. His choice was certain death if he stayed, and probable death if he jumped. He chose the option with minimal probability for survival, even though it meant jumping into a dark sea with flames on top and freezing water below; and it meant breaking the ingrained rule of "never jump."

Stakeholder Analysis

Stakeholders	Level of support for the change	Level of impact change will have
Marketing	Support/proactive	LOW
Senior Management	Active support/ proactive	HIGH
Unions	Resistance	HIGH

YOUR TURN

Describe an important event in your organization. This event can be unexpected or anticipated, positive or negative. What demands is this change creating for your people? How will it change their lives?

What would be an example of an ingrained message, or belief, in your organization that would preclude people from "jumping off the burning platform" and that might create negative consequences? One example might be "never collaborate with a competitor" or "never trust

_____."

Step B.
Identify feelings and beliefs

- **What it means:**
    — Labeling the experience
- **How it works:**
    — Acknowledge feelings
    — Help people make positive choices on the feelings

The Idea

Identifying how a person feels requires the ability to label the inner experience in relation to what's happening.

Most events that create a demand for change bring about strong feelings. A death in the family may call forth uncontrollable feelings of grief, while a change in work responsibilities may bring out feelings of excitement and/or fear. If we don't experience these feelings, acknowledge them and utilize them, the repressed feelings will prevent us from making necessary changes. This repression may even cause us to act irrationally or develop physical symptoms of illness.

Managers need to observe and identify feelings among their employees and provide an environment where it feels safe to express them. Use the table of feeling words on the next page to help you identify how your employees may be feeling about the event you described on page 150.

Example

We are constantly in the process of describing events in our daily lives and trying to discern how we feel and what we believe about them. Unfortunately, the way we describe the events and the way we perceive the events frequently leads to unfavorable outcomes.

Albert Ellis, a famous cognitive psychologist, has developed a simple model for understanding this process. He calls the model an ABC approach in which:

A = Activating Experience
B = Belief System
C = Consequence

For example, the (A) activating experience might be that you are participating in a matrixed organization with two bosses that assume they own 100 percent of your time. The (C) consequence could be that you feel hopelessly overwhelmed and frazzled. Even though working in a matrixed virtual world does present challenges, part of the "frazzled" consequence may be your (B) belief that you must please both bosses perfectly all of the time.

While it is unlikely that you would be able to change the (A) activating experience, you may be able to change the (B) belief system accounting for a major share of the problem.

Feeling Words				
Happy	**Sad**	**Angry**	**Afraid**	**Confused**
Ecstatic	Suicidal	Alienated	Terrified	Disoriented
Thrilled	Despondent	Furious	Petrified	Shocked
Joyful	Depressed	Enraged	Panicky	Bewildered
Happy	Lonely	Resentful	Scared	Conflicted
Pleased	Sad	Frustrated	Afraid	Torn
Delighted	Unhappy	Aggravated	Anxious	Lost
Content	Blue	Mad	Timid	Unsure
Satisfied	Upset	Irritated	Cautious	Hesitant
OK	Concerned	Annoyed	Uneasy	Mixed-Up
Curious	Isolated		Intimidated	Overwhelmed

**YOUR
TURN**

*Think about a change that is affecting you personally and
identify some of the feelings and beliefs you are having
about that change.*

*Using the ABC model to deepen your understanding, how
might your belief system impact your feelings?*

Practicing a New Skill.
*Over the next week, take note of unexpected or antici-
pated events in your organization. Take time to identify the
event, describe it, understand its significance and listen to
the feelings you are observing in relation to the events.*

Skill 9:
Facilitate Acceptance of What Cannot Be Changed

- **Definition:** Helping employees accept that things will never be the same
- **Benefits:**
    - — Increases serenity
    - — Prepares to move on
- **Steps:**
    - A. Moving to commitment
    - B. Putting the past behind

Introduction

There are many things we can't change in life. They are irreversible: the process of growing old and dying, the inevitable demands of life transitions, and the appearance of disease, disruption and disaster. Whether in our personal lives or our work lives, events change us or the world around us. They may challenge our assumptions about the organization and ourselves. The nature of the event says we can't go on the way we have been. If we are going to make a healthy response to change, we must accept the event and its meaning before we can move on. The challenge is to accept the fact that the world is not the way we thought it was. Most people respond to change with some form of resistance. Much of the resistance we encounter comes from fear, mistrust, confusion, not understanding the need for change or comfort with the status quo. Managers need to recognize resistance for what it is, and learn to work with it.

Facilitating acceptance is the second task in our model for managing change. The goal of this step is to help your employees incorporate the following Serenity Prayer into their life:

> *Grant me the Serenity*
> *to Accept the things I cannot change,*
> *the Courage to change the things I can,*
> *and the Wisdom to know the difference.*

When a person can't, or won't, understand what has happened, acceptance is very difficult. It's hard enough to accept the negative changes in life, even when a person understands what has happened. Accepting it means that the clock cannot be turned back, no matter how much the person hopes and wishes. It doesn't mean they forget, but it does mean they go on. In this section, you will learn to facilitate two changes in attitude.

Step A. Moving to commitment.
Step B. Putting the past behind.

Step A.
Moving to commitment

- **What it means:**
  — Letting the event sink in emotionally and
     intellectually
- **How it works:**
  — Denial
  — Anger
  — Bargaining
  — Depression
  — Acceptance

The Idea

Moving to commitment is the ability to let the event sink
in emotionally and intellectually. In our model for making
a healthy response to change, understanding is the first
step. In the unhealthy response, resistance is the first
step. It is important to note that sometimes a person may
not be able to move to acceptance right away. Elizabeth
Kübler-Ross, a well-known author on managing change,
suggests a five-stage process for accepting loss:

- Denial
- Anger
- Bargaining
- Depression
- Acceptance

These five stages represent a grief and mourning process
resulting from feelings of abandonment and/or loss. All
grief and mourning is about severed relationships. Grief is
the feeling of loss at the interrupted or broken connection.
Mourning is the process of incorporating that loss into our
lives. While these phases are normally considered in

relation to loss, they can also apply to any turning point in life. Managers need to recognize these stages so that they can identify where people are in the process. Understanding that this is a process can help managers gently nudge people through the phases. If a person is in the anger stage, it doesn't mean that they won't get to acceptance. A manager should never give up on someone just because they seem to be exhibiting anger, depression or denial.

Denial is a defense against the reality of loss or change. The first reaction may be a temporary state of shock. After this initial feeling of numbness, the usual response is, "No, this can't be happening to me." This is a normal response to an abnormal situation. Getting stuck in the denial phase changes this normal response to an unhealthy response.

Anger is often the response to the question, "Why me?" In the denial phase, the first reaction is, "No, it's not true." Eventually this reaction gives way to the reality, "Oh yes, it is me." In many cases anger is displaced in several directions. Suddenly, no one can do anything right, nobody understands or cares. At some point, a person must look inward and understand the real source of the anger— losing control, losing dignity and giving up unfulfilled dreams. Anger, when properly directed, can be healthy. Sometimes there is a right to be angry.

Bargaining is an attempt to postpone. Usually it involves bargaining with a higher authority. There is a promise of good behavior in exchange for a postponement of the inevitable. At this stage of the transition process, there is a shift in the way the event is viewed. The event is real, but maybe it can be modified.

Depression is recognizing that a loss has occurred or will occur. Going through the sadness and despair of this phase paves the way for acceptance. It is part of the mourning process for the loss of meaningful people and places. It is also during this stage of the transition process that a search begins for new ways of viewing the world.

Depression that is like a deep sadness provides a doorway to transition. If the depression becomes "clinical," more like hopelessness, then there is a danger of being trapped.

Acceptance is the contemplation of an impending event with quiet expectation. In the acceptance phase, rest is not a resigned and hopeless giving up; it is a time of preparation and peace. Usually acceptance is preceded by an emotional "thud." The "thud" is the emotional realization of what has happened. The moment can feel like a bolt of lightning, when acceptance comes unexpectedly, or it can come as a gentle awakening when the acceptance process has been gradual. At this time, recycling the understanding skills can be very helpful.

Most of us have experienced all five phases of the grief and mourning process (denial, anger, bargaining, depression and acceptance) in relation to certain changes in our lives. The sequence may be different for different people and your associates may not pass through all phases. People may also recycle through certain stages as they work toward acceptance.

Example
Try to identify the five stages of grief that an employee experiences as she moves toward acceptance of an office closing.

When Karen first heard about the office closing, she wouldn't tell her family or friends. She didn't want to deal with her own feelings about the change, let alone others' feelings about it. A week later she told her family and they too began the process of acceptance.

Karen felt resentful and angry at her supervisors and the unknown "decision-makers" at the parent company. For a day or so, she tried to convince her supervisor that the office didn't need to be closed, and promised to work harder. Always a team player, Karen now resented taking direction from her supervisors. It became increasingly difficult to get up in the morning. She lost interest in looking nice for work. She came to work late and left early.

Her family was pressuring her to find another job, but Karen just couldn't get up the energy to look. After several months, Karen experienced the emotional "thud" of her change when co-workers expressed excitement at finding new job opportunities. Karen started to accept the fact that her life had changed. With the support of her family, she began to think about new possibilities and what she might like to do in a new job.

YOUR TURN

In relation to the event you described on page 150, how have your associates experienced each of the five phases leading to acceptance? Describe the feelings and the reasons for those feelings. If you did not notice a phase, leave that space blank.

The event (summary):

Denial:

Anger:

Bargaining:

Depression:

Acceptance:

Where are your people now in the transition process?

Step B.
Putting the past behind

- **What it means:**
  — Accepting the past without being trapped in it
- **How it works:**
  — Gaining perspective
  — Shedding the old image

The Idea

Putting the past behind involves accepting the past without being trapped by it. Accepting means more than letting the event sink in emotionally; it also means letting go. Letting go is a way to recognize that acceptance of the "new" means that something of the "old" must go. Getting the past behind takes time and often includes a recycling of the acceptance and understanding processes.

Often before we can put the past behind us, we have to gain perspective. Gaining perspective means getting some distance, or detachment, from the event. Getting distance helps break up the old cue-system that served to reinforce roles and to pattern behavior. With distance, people feel free to let go.

During this stage of the change process it is helpful for managers to be a bit more flexible with people and to relax the controls. Because there may be ambiguity, managers need to let people find their way and suggest alternatives.

Once we have gained perspective, the next step is to shed the old image, which requires breaking some familiar connections to the world. This can take the form of roles, behaviors and identity. It may also require challenging beliefs about the organization and letting go of illusions that are getting in the way of efforts to change. Often during times of transition, people will have feelings of not being sure of who they are any more or who they are working for. In some sense, they may find themselves in a state of limbo, between the old identity and the new identity or situation. Letting go of prior images that defined the organization, if only temporarily, is a critical step in putting the old behind you.

Managers need to look at how the norms and behaviors of the organization may be changing.

Example
Karen had to reflect about the coming change. For 20 years her image of herself was attached to her job and her company. Now she had to let go of that identity without really having a new identity to replace it. She felt a little lost. Fortunately, her manager understood Karen's loss. She was given the space to shed the old image, before high expectations were placed on her.

YOUR TURN

How is the event you described on page 150 creating demands for your staff to change? Use the space below to describe how you might be able to get the old ways behind and increase readiness to make a transition.

What people have to let go of:

What the new image is:

SKILL 10:
ENABLE CHANGE

- **Definition:** Preparing and moving to something new
- **Benefits:**
  - — Seeing opportunity
  - — Gaining direction
- **Steps:**
  - A. Making the transition
  - B. Beginning again

Introduction

Gail Sheehy, in her book *Passages,* compares humans to lobsters. The lobster grows by developing and shedding a series of hard protective shells. Each time it expands from within, the confining shell must be discarded. The lobster is left exposed and vulnerable until, in time, a new covering grows to replace the old.

And so it is with us. Getting the past behind means shedding a protective structure that is really not functional anymore. We are left exposed and vulnerable, but also fresh and challenged, capable of stretching in ways we hadn't known before. This shedding may take several years or more. If we don't shed our defensive shells, life will become stifling and uncomfortable. In our heart we know we must change. Yet, questions such as "What should we do?" and "What can we do?" still challenge and frighten us.

The third step in our Managing Change model is Enabling Change. This section will present two steps to help your people make a new beginning:

Step A. Making the transition.
Step B. Beginning again.

Step A.
Making the transition

- **What it means:**
  - Finding something useful in the emptiness or pain created by letting go of the past
- **How it works:**
  - Discover what's left
  - Understand the pitfalls
  - Settle into the reality of moving forward

The Idea
Making the transition involves the ability to find something useful in the emptiness or pain created by letting go of the past. The gap between acceptance and beginning again can be a time of considerable disorientation.

Change means heading into unfamiliar territory. A person's foundation and sense of direction may get lost. They might feel confused. Ordinary things may seem unreal, and what used to seem critically important may suddenly lose value. Out of this disorientation, a person struggles for some direction. The key to finding that direction is to confront the feeling of "emptiness." Help people find something useful in any change being made.

Making the transition may be a time for exploration and experimentation. While the new reality is sinking in, encourage people to remain open to new possibilities.

To begin making the transition we have to discover what remains in the aftermath of a life-changing or work-changing event. Finding the positive in the emotional aftermath is a test of inner resources and faith.

It is important during this step to provide sufficient time for an inner reorientation to the change. Review old commitments and exercise caution in making new ones. Don't rush this inner process. Give people time. They may be tempted to act for the sake of action, but those actions often lead to trouble.

It should be a time to reflect on past experiences and let new desires emerge. The desires that emerge in the transition period are an important part of discovering what's left. In fact, they may be a large share of what is left.

People need to take good care of themselves during this transition. Encourage them to exercise and eat right. It is equally important to attend to emotional needs. Find resources for your people to talk to. That person can be a caring friend or a trained professional. Getting needed support is part of taking good care of themselves.

Five Traps

Often when people are working through to new beginnings they may fall into five cognitive traps. Most of these traps are a result of being torn between the old and the new. Managers need to recognize these traps that can get in the way of successful change.

The five traps to making a successful transition are:

- Moving too quickly in an attempt to remove the emptiness.
- Becoming defensive and impatient because transition time feels unproductive.
- Becoming depressed about changing of old patterns.
- Letting fear get in the way of a deeper understanding.
- Making rapid "adjustments" to overcome feelings of being overwhelmed.

A person needs to avoid becoming so immobilized by the old that they can't enter into the emptiness and learn what it has to offer. People need to stay in the emptiness long enough to discover new possibilities.

Readiness to Change Indicators

People will get to a sense of readiness to make changes. Here are four indicators of readiness to move forward:

- People are not recycling as much. They spend less emotional energy on the past and stop reviewing what should or shouldn't have been done.

- People feel an inner stirring to make a commitment to move ahead. They spend more emotional energy around the new image they are creating for themselves. And they connect socially with new peers.

- People have a clearer vision of where to go. A new vision of possibilities starts to emerge that gives them a sense of direction.

- People start to integrate the change into their reality. They'll start thinking, saying and doing things that demonstrate a commitment to the change.

When you start noticing these readiness indicators, you will know that people are starting to settle into the reality of moving forward. They are moving out of the transition phase and beginning again to build a new reality.

YOUR TURN

What are some of the positive things that could come out of the changes?

What is left for the people?

What pitfalls have you found employees falling into during the transition?

What readiness indicators have you noticed that let you know your people are settling into the reality of moving forward?

Step B.
Beginning again

- **What it means:**
  - Acting on the desire to make something happen
- **How it works:**
  - Set a goal
  - Choose a strategy
  - Develop support

The Idea

Beginning again means acting on the desire to make something happen. Understanding without action is fairly useless. Once people have reached a point of readiness to act, it is important to encourage action. Acceptance decreases the chances of going through the future anchored to the past. Making the transition increases the chances of creating a new vision of what's possible. Beginning again gets people moving forward again to implement and live with the change. This involves setting a goal, choosing a strategy and developing support.

Setting a goal means developing some direction in the change process. Setting a goal gives people a way to measure progress.

Choosing a strategy is helping people select the best alternative for achieving their goals. To give people the best chance of success, help them select a strategy that best matches their style.

Developing support means mobilizing whatever resources are needed to increase your employees' chances for success. This may require exploring some new lifestyle possibilities, including exercise, stress management, healthy eating or quitting smoking. Providing training, education and other physical and emotional support develops a positive outlook among employees. It may also mean involving other people in the change program to support them in a new beginning. You may want to reward progress or help people get back on track when they experience setbacks.

Example

Karen's goal: I will learn new job skills to give myself greater opportunities for a new position. I will learn computer skills to make me eligible to work at home as part of a virtual team.

Karen's strategy for change: I will enroll in the skills training course offered by the company.

Karen's support: I will ask my family to help with chores and to respect my need for study time.

YOUR TURN

In the space below, please complete the following statements for one person you are helping to begin again.

The goal is:

The strategy is:

The support will be:

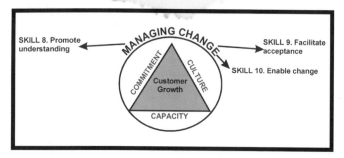

Task IV. Managing Change Exercise

In this task, you learned three skills to help you manage change within your organization:

- Promote understanding
- Facilitate acceptance
- Enable change

Please review these three skills and decide what actions you can take in your organization to manage change.

Task IV. Summary

This task presented a healthy response to managing change in turbulent times. It was designed to give you some insights and tools for helping your employees let go of illusions, accept their realities and focus on the possibilities even when working in a virtual world of geographically dispersed teams.

The first section demonstrated how you could promote understanding of the event, the demands that it created and how people felt about it. It is vitally important, especially in virtual teams situations, that people have a full understanding of the changes taking place.

The second section helped you facilitate acceptance of what cannot be changed. You learned some ways to help people move toward commitment, gain perspective and shed their old image. This process enables people to experience the reality of the change and to let it sink in emotionally as well as intellectually.

The third section focused on helping people change what they can so that they can invest their energy into new beginnings. You helped people set goals and develop strategies to reach those goals.

If you understand change and facilitate a healthy response to the changes people face in life, you will make a significant contribution to organizational and individual health. Remember to pay attention to the signs of mismanaging change: denying, repressing and stagnating. We hope that these skills for managing change will lead to new opportunities for your people.

SUMMARY

- Mobilize people behind the shared values, strategy and structure
- Empower people
- Recognize individual and team contributions
- Develop people
- Create a learning organization
- Articulate the cultural requirements for success
- Create a cultural revolution
- Promote understanding
- Facilitate acceptance
- Enable change

As organizations experience the turbulence caused by the great pace of changes happening in our world, many will be aware of what is happening and take steps to engage in a systematic changing corporate culture effort.

Although a great master plan can be created for corporate culture change, commitment, capacity, alignment of the culture, and managing the process of change are necessary for success. Maximizing employee commitment involves mobilizing employees behind the new values and vision of the organization. This is done by defining and communicating the vision, mission, goals, objectives and values of the organization and by empowering people with direction, autonomy and necessary support. In addition, reward systems specifically targeted to the individual motivators that reward the behaviors required by the new values and vision will facilitate the shifting of employee attitudes.

Building capacity within the organization involves developing people by attending to the physical, intellectual, emotional and spiritual health of the employees. By creating a learning organization of empowered, energized and committed people, the new vision for the organization begins to take shape.

Leaders must ensure that the corporate culture is not only in tandem with the new vision and values but also in support of technology-enabled virtual work. Not only do we have to "talk the talk, but we have to walk the walk." Articulating the values and translating those into more concrete norms and behaviors ensures that the new vision is not just talk and that virtual work is for real. Creating this type of environment may require a cultural revolution. If we choose to engage in radical thinking and revolutionary ideas, we need to be thoughtful and deliberate. It requires a systematic process that takes full advantage of technologies that deal with distance and people skills to deal with diversity.

Revolution should never be considered lightly. Yet, the business drivers that we discussed in the introduction impose demands on organizational leaders that may require revolutionary thoughts and ways of doing business. The whole nature of relationships with customers, competitors and suppliers has changed. Technology and team demographics have caused alterations in organizational dynamics that we could not have anticipated even a decade earlier. Radical changes require radical solutions.

In this book, you have learned ten skills to help you maximize commitment, build capacity, align the culture, and manage change. Hopefully, these skills will help you navigate the changes thrust upon you in mindful and productive ways. By living in the questions we have introduced here, you have begun to develop your action plan for renewal.

Bibliography

Argyris, Chris. "Good Communication That Blocks Learning." *Harvard Business Review,* July/August 1994, Pg. 77.

Antonini, Joseph E. "Organizational Renewal is More Than a New Logo." *Journal of Business Strategy,* January/February 1994. Clippings: Pg. 12, 266 words, Essay, Focus on Renewal. College Station, Texas: Arthur Anderson & Co. and Center for Retailing Studies, Texas A&M University, 1994.

Beckhard, Richard and Harris, Reuben, T. *Organizational Transitions.* Boston: Addison-Wesley Publishing, 1987.

Bellingham, Richard and Cohen, Barry. *Ethical Leadership: A Competitive Edge.* Amherst, MA. Human Resource Development Press, 1990.

Bellingham, Richard and Cohen, Barry. *Leadership Myths and Realities.* Amherst, MA: Human Resource Development Press, 1989.

Bellingham, Richard and Cohen, Barry. *The Corporate Wellness Sourcebook.* Amherst, MA: Human Resource Development Press, 1987.

Bellingham, Richard and Cohen, Barry et al. *The Corporate Culture Sourcebook.* Amherst, MA: Human Resource Development Press, 1990.

Bellingham, Richard; Tager, Mark; and Elias, Walter. *Designing Effective Health Promotion Programs.* Amherst, MA: Human Resource Development Press, 1991.

Carkhuff, Robert R. *Empowering the Creative Leader.* Amherst, MA: Human Resource Development Press, 1989.

Carkhuff, Robert R. *The Age of the New Capitalism.* Amherst, MA: Human Resource Development Press, 1988.

Carkhuff, Robert R. *Interdependence.* Amherst, MA: Human Resource Development Press, 1992.

Carkhuff, Robert R. *The Exemplar.* Amherst, MA: Human Resource Development Press, 1984.

Carkhuff, Robert R. *Human Processing and Human Productivity.* Amherst, MA: Human Resource Development Press, 1986.

Carkhuff, Robert R. *Sources of Human Productivity.* Amherst, MA: Human Resource Development Press, 1983.

Davidow, William H. and Malone, Michael S. *The Virtual Corporation: Structuring and Revitalizing the Corporation for the 21st Century.* New York: Harper Collins, 1992.

Greiner, Ray and Metes, George. *Going Virtual.* Upper Saddle River, NJ: Prentice-Hall, 1995.

Guy, Mary. *From Organizational Decline to Organizational Renewal.* New York: Quorum Books, 1989.

Handy, Charles B. *The Age of Paradox.* Boston: Harvard Business School Press, 1994.

Hastings, Colin. *The New Organization: Growing the Culture of Organizational Networking.* London: McGraw-Hill, 1993.

Hsieh, Tsun-Yan. "The Road to Renewal: Organizational Management." *The McKinsey Quarterly,* June 22, 1992, No. 3, Pg. 28.

Hurst, David K. *Crisis & Renewal: Meeting the Challenge of Organizational Change.* Boston: Harvard Business School Press, 1995.

Hutchinson, Colin. *Vitality and Renewal: A Manager's Guide for the 21st Century.* Westport, CT: Praeger, 1995.

Hutt, Michael D.; Walker, Beth A.; Frankwick, Gary L. "Hurdle the Cross-Functional Barriers to Strategic Change." *Sloan Management Review,* March 22, 1995, Vol. 36, No. 3, Pg. 22.

Kotter, John P. and Heskett, James L. *Corporate Culture and Performance.* New York: The Free Press, 1992.

Lippit, Gordon L. *Organizational Renewal.* Englewood Cliffs, NJ: Prentice-Hall, 1982.

Lorenz, Christopher. "New Light on the Grail of Corporate Renewal." *Financial Times,* August 12, 1994, Friday, Management; Pg. 9.

McLennan, Roy. *Managing Organizational Change.* Englewood Cliffs, NJ: Prentice-Hall, 1989.

Mink, Oscar G. *Change at Work: A Comprehensive Management Process for Transforming Organizations.* San Francisco: Jossey-Bass, 1993.

Scrivner, Stephen A.R. *Computer-Supported Cooperative Work.* Aldershot Avebury Technical, 1994.

Spender, J.C. and Grinyer, P.H. "Organizational Renewal: Top Management's Role in a Loosely Coupled System." *Human Relations,* August 1995, Vol. 48, No. 8, Pg. 909. Special Issue: Corporate Governance and Control.

Spurr, Kathy. *Computer Support for Co-Operative Work.* West Sussex, England: John Wiley & Sons, 1994.

Index